secrets OF
iLumina™

by Randy Peterson & Jeremy Taylor

discover it ➔

TYNDALE HOUSE PUBLISHERS, INC.
WHEATON, ILLINOIS

Visit Tyndale's exciting Web site at www.tyndale.com or get news and updates on
iLumina at www.iLumina.com.

Copyright © 2003 by Tyndale House Publishers. All rights reserved.

Cover photo copyright © 2003 by Visual Book Productions, Inc. All rights reserved.

Written by Randy Petersen and Jeremy P. Taylor.

Designed by Dean H. Renninger.

Unless otherwise indicated, all Scripture quotations are taken from the *Holy Bible,*
New Living Translation, copyright © 1996. Used by permission of Tyndale House
Publishers, Inc., Wheaton, Illinois 60189. All rights reserved.

ISBN 0-8423-8615-7

Printed in the United States of America.

07 06 05 04 03
6   5   4   3

iLumina is a trademark of Tyndale House Publishers, Inc.

Microsoft and Windows are registered trademarks of Microsoft Corporation in the
United States and/or other countries.

Mac and QuickTime are registered trademarks of Apple Computer, Inc.

Adobe and Acrobat are registered trademarks of Adobe Systems Incorporated.
Macromedia is a trademark of Macromedia, Inc.

⊕ CONTENTS

◉ PART II: SURFING THE SCREENS

WELCOME TO *ILUMINA*

MAYBE YOU'VE ALREADY been exploring the nooks and crannies of *iLumina* on your own, or maybe you're just firing up the software now. In any case, you're probably figuring out that *iLumina* is unlike anything you've ever seen. *iLumina* is not just a computerized Bible. It's not just a Bible reference library on computer. It's an experience that will draw you in to the biblical world—and it might just change your life.

That's not just ad hype—it's the first secret of *iLumina*: *To use this software to its fullest potential, you need to* experience *it.* Dig into it. Play with it—knock around the streets of Jerusalem; stand with David as he slays Goliath; figure out five ways 1 Corinthians applies to your morning routine. "Live the Bible." That's the slogan our marketing experts came up with, and they got it exactly right. If your Bible's been getting a bit dusty lately, take this one for a ride. It will take you places you've never dreamed of.

Here are three things you need to know about *iLumina* up front.

It's **visual.** If you just want to read words on a screen, you've come to the wrong place. Oh, there are plenty of words here, but here you'll see the biblical story unfolding in state-of-the art animations, timelines, charts, maps, and photos—not to mention the incredibly innovative Virtual Tours and Points in Time, where you can actually move through biblical scenes as if you were there.

It's **interactive.** You are traveling through time. You are strolling through the tabernacle. You are joining the disciples in the upper room. And it's all interconnected. You're always just a click away from a new adventure.

It's **practical.** The Bible says God's Word is "a message to obey, not just to listen to" (James 1:22). There's a lot to learn here, but true Bible learning has to involve your whole life, not just your brain. By incorporating the resources of the *Life Application Bible*, *iLumina* offers news you can use.

The stated mission of *iLumina* is printed right there on the package. As we write this book, it's a mission we're happy to join.

OUR MISSION

The producers of iLumina *aim to enhance your understanding of the Bible and make it fun and exciting. We want you to be able to enter the world of the Bible in a thrilling new way.*

USING THIS BOOK

All sorts of people are using *iLumina*, and that means all sorts of people are reading this book. Maybe you're a computer expert, always looking for the latest innovations. Or maybe you just got a computer for Christmas and it's still pretty new to you. Maybe you've been studying the Bible all your life. Or maybe this program is your introduction to those ancient texts. Maybe you're preaching sermons, teaching Sunday school, leading a youth group, or writing papers on biblical themes. Or maybe you simply read the Bible for your personal enrichment, in the quiet of your own home.

We're writing this book for all of the above.

If you're a computer whiz, forgive us for the basic level of the instructions we give. We don't mean to insult your intelligence; we figure you can skip over those parts. And if you're a Bible whiz, some of our Bible study examples might seem pretty basic, but we think you'll find *iLumina*'s tools and wealth of information useful for deeper study as well.

As you read, you can become part of *iLumina*'s development team. If you find your own secrets in *iLumina* or have tips on how to use *iLumina* better, please go to www.iLumina.com. Use the tech support page to email us. We want you to be our partner as we push back the limits of Bible software and continue to develop the world's first digitally animated Bible and encyclopedia suite.

Please also note that in this book we have followed a couple of conventions for the sake of clarity. The first is that we have occasionally marked some features of *iLumina* with an asterisk (*). Features followed by an asterisk exist only in *iLumina Gold,* and not in *iLumina*. Also, where a menu item, icon, or button is referred to that links to another screen, it is in bold (e.g. **ENCYCLOPEDIA** or **NLT & KJV SIDE-BY-SIDE**).

THE FEATURES OF THIS BOOK

People approach a computer program differently. Some like to play with it. They jump into a program and start clicking things. *What does this do?* They want to know the structure of the program, what connects with what. But others don't care how the program is constructed. They want to know how to use it. *How can I do this?*

We've designed our two main sections around these two approaches.

PART 1: USING *ILUMINA*

We call this the "verb" approach. It's all about *doing* this or that. Reading the Bible. Consulting study aids. Looking things up in the Encyclopedia. You can look through the Table of Contents or just flip through the book and find instructions for the things you want to do.

PART 2: SURFING THE SCREENS

If you want to poke around the program and see what each screen does, this is the section you want. With pictures of each screen, it will identify each nook and cranny, helping you understand *iLumina* as well as its programmers do—maybe better.

Whatever sections you use, we hope this book will answer your questions as you use this amazing program. We also hope it will inspire and enable you to squeeze every possible advantage out of *iLumina*. And maybe we can all have some fun in the process.

DISCOVERING *ILUMINA*

You'll also notice another feature spread throughout this book, which we call "Discovering *iLumina*." These are a variety of stories designed to give you, our readers, practical ideas about how *iLumina* can be used in any number of situations. You'll read stories about pastors, small group leaders, teens—people of all sorts.

INSTALLING *ILUMINA*

You're holding a state-of-the-art Bible resource. With these few discs, your computer can become a valuable tool of instruction and inspiration, of worship and witness. So let's get started.

As we prepared this book, we were calling the Discovering *iLumina* feature "Real-Life Examples." Then we realized something: *We're making these stories up.* **So, although they're not real-life examples in the truest sense of the phrase, they are realistic examples of how people might** *really* **use *iLumina*. Really!**

SYSTEM REQUIREMENTS

To run *iLumina*, these are the minimum system requirements:

For Windows Users
- Pentium III or higher processor
- Microsoft Windows 98, Windows 2000 professional, Windows Me, or Windows XP operating system
- 128 MB of RAM (256 MB recommended)

For Mac Users
- Mac OS X v 10.2
- 256 MB of RAM

For All Users
- 520 MB of available hard disk space (2.4 GB hard disk space for "copy-to-hard-drive" installation for faster access)
- Quad-speed or faster CD-ROM drive (or DVD-ROM to run *iLumina* from DVD)
- Super VGA monitor and video card, supporting 1024 x 768 resolution, 16-bit color or higher
- Mouse or compatible pointing device
- Sound card and speakers
- Adobe Reader version 5.0 or higher (included)
- QuickTime 6.3 (included)
- Printer (optional but recommended)

THE SOFTWARE PACKAGE

The *iLumina* program is contained in four CD-ROM discs or one DVD-ROM disc. You have all five discs in the *iLumina* package, but you won't need all five. If your computer has a DVD-ROM drive, you only need the one DVD-ROM disc. If your computer has only a CD-ROM drive, you need only the four CD-ROM discs. The extra disc makes a dandy coaster.

Do not try to play the DVD-ROM disc in your DVD player. It won't work, and it might make something explode. Okay, we're just kidding about the explosion, but a normal DVD player won't play this disc. You need a DVD-ROM drive on your computer.

NOTE

Just so there's no confusion: *the same program* that's on the single DVD is also on the four CDs. (Obviously, a DVD holds a lot more data than a CD.) So, even if you don't have a DVD-ROM on your computer, you won't miss anything in *iLumina*.

INSTALLING *ILUMINA* FROM CD-ROM

1. Exit all programs running on your computer.
2. Place Disc 1, the "Installation Disc", in your CD-ROM drive. If your computer is using the Autorun feature, the next few steps might happen automatically. But if nothing happens, proceed to steps 3 and 4.

3. Click on the START menu, and click on the RUN command. That will open the RUN dialog box.
4. Type **D:\setup.exe** and click OK. (Most CD-ROM drives are labeled "D," but some have other letters. Use the correct drive letter for your system.)
5. Follow the instructions on screen. You will be prompted to eject the first disc and insert the next three CD-ROM discs at their proper times.

INSTALLING *ILUMINA* FROM DVD-ROM

1. Exit all programs running on your computer.
2. Place the *iLumina* DVD in your DVD-ROM drive. If your computer is using the Autorun feature, the next few steps might happen automatically. But if nothing happens, proceed to steps 3 and 4.
3. Click on the START menu, and click on the RUN command. That will open the RUN dialog box.
4. Type **D:\setup.exe** and click OK. (Your DVD-ROM drive might be labeled "E" or something else. Use the correct drive letter for your system.)
5. Follow the instructions on screen.

INSTALLATION ON A MAC

1. Exit all running applications.
2. Place Disc 1, the "Installation Disc", in your CD-ROM drive, or place the DVD in your DVD-ROM drive.
3. If the Installation Disc or DVD does not open, double-click on it to open the disc's contents.
4. Double-click the icon named "iLumina Install" or "iLumina Gold Install."
5. Follow the instructions on screen to complete the installation, ejecting and inserting the successive CDs as necessary.

STARTING *ILUMINA*

After you install *iLumina* successfully, it should be listed on your Program menu. Click on **ILUMINA** and then **ILUMINA BIBLE** should appear. Click on that, and the program should begin. If you are using a Mac, the *iLumina* icon will be in your Applications folder, unless you chose a different directory during install.

During installation, you were asked whether you wanted an *iLumina* icon on your desktop. If you said yes, then there's a blue **ILUMINA BIBLE** starburst sitting there on your screen. Click on that and the program will fire up.

Now, on *iLumina*'s home page you will be confronted by an ugly Philistine giant—don't be alarmed; David took care of him. And you'll see a rainbow of options presented to you— the five or six different sections of *iLumina*. Click on any of these names to go to the Welcome screen for that section. If this is your first time using *iLumina*, we suggest you start where this book starts, with **THE BIBLE**.

PART 1

using
ILumina →

CHAPTER ONE

→ NAVIGATING *ILUMINA*

BEFORE YOU TAKE *iLumina* for a spin around the block, get to know the dashboard. Virtually every screen of this program has three strips at the top that will take you where you want to go.

THE MENU BAR

iLumina has six main sections, appearing on the first screen that you see when you boot up the program (We'll refer to this as *iLumina*'s home page in the future). These are also displayed all the time in the menu bar, just under the section title across the top of each screen.

`:: THE BIBLE  :: ENCYCLOPEDIA  :: TIME TRAVEL  :: MEDIA CENTER  :: EXTRAS  :: MY STUDY CENTER`

At any time, you can click on one of those titles in the menu bar, and you'll be able to enter the various screens in that particular section. Only in the full-screen Theater Mode is the menu bar hidden, but you can easily see it again by clicking the **BACK** arrow in the upper right corner of the screen.

THE SEARCH BAR

Just under the menu bar, you'll see another strip with some empty spaces, or text boxes, built in. That's the Search bar. Just type in a word or name, or perhaps a Bible book or chapter, and click **GO**. It will then search for whatever you've typed and take you there.

The **FIND** space at the left of the Search bar conducts a search of the *immediate surroundings*. It's like searching for a misplaced letter on your messy desk. So, if you're in the Bible section and you want to locate a certain word or phrase *in your current chapter,* type it in, and the word or phrase will appear in

GOING FOR THE GOLD
Why don't I have all this stuff in my *iLumina 2.0?*

While adding lots of cool programming to *iLumina* and creating *iLumina Gold,* the makers wanted to maintain a version that would be affordable for everyone. That's *iLumina 2.0.* It's a very nice program, but it lacks some of the features of the Gold edition. Throughout this book, we'll mark with an asterisk things that apply only to *iLumina Gold.*

bold or in red, depending on your choice in **OPTIONS.** In the Encyclopedia, it will search the current article. (To learn about removing the front style or color, see "Changing the size of the Bible Text" in chapter two.)

But say you're searching for all the info you can get on Forgiveness or Corinth or Transportation. Type it into the **SEARCH** box (second from left), and the program will rifle through all of *iLumina*, or just a particular section, to find what you want. It will generate a list of entries for your perusal.

The GO TO space can read any reasonable abbreviation of a Bible book, and any punctuation between chapter and verse. So Genesis 50:10 could be abbreviated as Gn 50.10 or Gen 50,10.

If you already know the Bible passage you want, use the **GO TO** box on any of the Bible screens. Type in the reference. Or just click on the down-arrow and you'll get a list of Bible books. Click on the one you want, and you'll get a list of chapters. Click on the chapter you want, and you'll get a list of verses. Click on the verse you want and—*voila!*—you're looking at it.

In *iLumina Gold*, you also have the choice of Bible translation.* Be sure the Version Selector on the right side of the Search bar is displaying the version you want, whether New Living Translation (NLT) or King James Version (KJV) or both the King James Version and New Living Translation (NLT & KJV).

THE TOOLBAR

To the right of the Search bar, you see nine buttons with strange symbols on them, symbols gleaned from ancient Aramaic grave markings. Clicked in the right sequence, these buttons will unleash the hidden power of *iLumina*! Ok, we're just kidding about the Aramaic grave markings (The smiley-face doesn't really look Aramaic, does it?), but these buttons certainly will supply you with some useful capabilities. Here are the true meanings of these not-so-ancient symbols.

 BACK takes you back to your previous screen.

 FORWARD brings you forward to where you were before you went back

 HOME takes you back to the Welcome screen of whatever section you're in. If you're in the Bible text, **HOME** takes you to the introduction to whatever book of the Bible you're in. Click it again to reach the Bible section Intro screen. Click it again to reach the *iLumina*'s home page.

SEARCH allows you to search all of *iLumina*, or part of it, for any word or phrase you want.

PRINT begins the process of printing the contents of your current screen. *Note: You won't get all the graphics, but the text should come through nicely.*

FAVORITES (yes, that's the smiley-face) will offer you a list of your preferred *iLumina* locations. If you're leading a 25-week study of Obadiah, for instance, you'll want to keep coming back to the Obadiah page. Just click the **FAVORITES** button, and click **ADD**. Then every time after that, Obadiah will be listed among your favorites, so just click **FAVORITES**, click Obadiah, and reap the prophet. (This is especially helpful if you're bouncing between three or more favorite screens, like the Bible text of Obadiah, the Encyclopedia entry on Obadiah, and the Atlas map of Edom. Add them all to **FAVORITES** and just click there.)

⊕ *Every screen in* iLumina *has three basic toolbars at the top.*

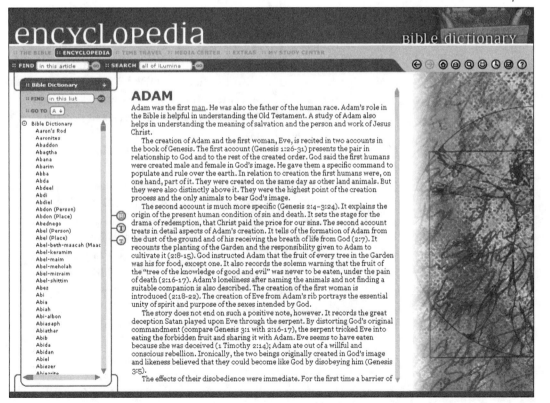

HISTORY offers a list of where you've been in *iLumina*. Click any of the listed entries and get back to where you once belonged. (The icon is a clock, showing three o'clock, which coincidentally is the exact time the programmers came up with that logo. In the morning.)

 OPTIONS (that's a checked box) will give you an opportunity to tailor *iLumina* to your particular needs and preferences.

If you always want to start from *iLumina*'s home page, you can choose to **SHOW MAIN MENU SCREEN**. It's a cool screen, but maybe you want to get right to work. In that case, select **GO DIRECTLY TO MODULE** and choose one of the six sections of *iLumina*, ideally the one you go to most often.

The **DEFAULT TRANSLATION** box will allow you to choose what translation is used when you click on a Scripture reference link. If you're using *iLumina Gold,* this means that when you click a link to a Bible verse in the Encyclopedia section, for instance, you could choose to have the verse appear in the King James Version.

The program is designed to **USE INTERFACE SOUNDS**— the little clicks and thumps you hear as you move the mouse over a command, or do some other navigation— but if these annoy you, you can uncheck that box.

You could also uncheck **SHOW TOOLTIPS**, but if you want to do that, you're too smart to be reading this anyway. Tooltips are the little explanations that pop up when you hold the pointer over a button for a few seconds.

If you check the box for **CONFIRM BEFORE JUMPING TO LINKS**, the program will prompt you whenever you click a link to a different screen of *iLumina*. "Jump to that article now?" it will ask you. And you will say, "Yes! That's exactly what I want to do! You got a problem with that?" Leave this unchecked, especially if you have self-esteem issues. You don't need that kind of second-guessing.

Unchecking the option to **SHOW BIBLE CHAPTERS IN GO TO MENU** will hide the submenu that shows the chapters in each Bible book on the **GO TO** menu. If you're a big fan of submenus and you like to use this to jump directly to specific chapters of the Bible books, you'll probably want to leave it checked.

On the right hand side of the dialog box you will notice three fairly standard buttons. Pressing **OK** will cause the program to accept your changes and close the dialog box, **CANCEL** will close the dialog box without accepting your changes, and **HELP** will display *iLumina*'s help files for your perusal.

Clicking the **MORE** button will display another dialog box with three other options to choose from. First, you have the option to **SHOW CONNECTING LINES IN TREE LISTS**. Selecting this will show the implicit connections in the hierarchical "tree" lists in the index windows (like the Bible Resource Index on the right side of the Bible Welcome screen). The next option is to **USE STANDARD TOOLTIP STYLE**. *iLumina*'s tooltips normally have a black background with white text; if you'd prefer you can use standard style, where tooltips have an off-white background with dark text. Lastly, you have the option to **SHOW 'FOUND' WORDS IN BOLD** or in **COLOR**. Choosing **COLOR** will show the words you search for with the **FIND** box in red instead of in bold. To return to the main Options dialog box from here just press the **BACK** button at the lower right.

⊕ *Clicking the Options button will bring up a dialog box where you can change* iLumina's *settings.*

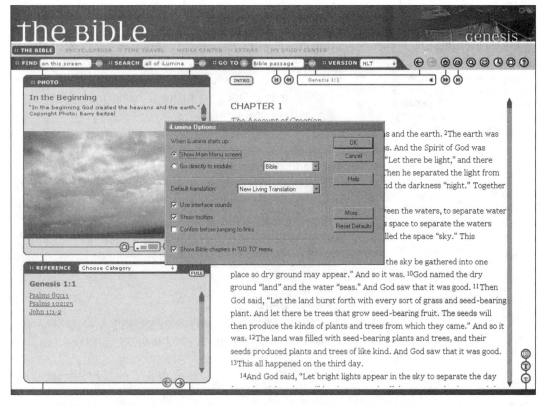

Back at the lower right of the main Options dialog box, you can press the **RESET DEFAULTS** button. If you've changed something here and don't like the results, press this button and everything will go back to square one—animated startup, sounds, tooltips, and no confirmation.

 HELP will take you to a place where all your questions will be answered—at least all your questions about *iLumina*. If you have an active Internet hookup, you can get help online, but a help screen will appear even if you're not online. There you can browse through the Contents of *iLumina*, click on the part of the screen you're wondering about, or look up a specific issue in the Index.

THE WINDOW CONTROLS

You know this already. Every computer program in the world has these. But just in case you've forgotten, let's talk about the buttons with the short line and the *X* in the top right corner of the screen. The button with the short line is the **MINIMIZE** button. It makes the program disappear temporarily, sending it to your taskbar if you're running Windows, or adding it to the Dock if you are running OS X. Just click the proper place on the taskbar or the Dock to bring it back, and you'll start right where you left off.

On *iLumina*'s closing screen, you'll notice credits for the creative people who developed, designed, and programmed *iLumina*. Press the ALT key and click on their names to reveal the personal messages and greetings some have hidden there.

The button with the *X* is the **CLOSE** button. When you're finished with *iLumina* for the day, click that and the program will close down. (Before closing down, you'll see a closing screen that lists all the lovely people who made *iLumina* possible, and gives you one last chance to return to *iLumina*. Click **EXIT NOW** if you're really finished.)

THE SALAD BAR

Begin by choosing iceberg, endive, or arugula, then click the garnish button . . . oh, wait, wrong program. Sorry.

CHAPTER TWO

➔ READING THE BIBLE

FROM THE *iLumina* home page, in order to read Bible text or look up verses, start by clicking on **THE BIBLE**.

You can also get to the Bible section from any other screen by clicking on **THE BIBLE** where it appears in the menu bar and choosing the specific screen you want.

The lower half of the opening screen of the Bible section has two headings: Bible Version and Bible Companions. To get right to the Bible text, click on the translation you prefer. That will take you to the first chapter of Genesis in that translation. We'll discuss Bible Companions later.

PICKING A BIBLE VERSION

iLumina Gold has two complete translations of the Bible: the New Living Translation (NLT) and the King James Version* (KJV). First-time Bible readers may wish to start with the NLT, since its format is more like reading a newspaper. The KJV, translated in 1611, is more poetic and classical, and might be more familiar to some users.

Clicking on either the **NEW LIVING TRANSLATION** or **KING JAMES VERSION** link will take you directly to that Bible text. Or, if you prefer, you can view both translations at once by clicking on the **NLT & KJV SIDE-BY-SIDE** link.

Note: iLumina *has only the NLT.*

LOOKING UP BIBLE VERSES

If you want to find a specific Bible verse, chapter, or book, you have several options.

The quickest is to use the Search bar. Type the reference into the **GO TO** box. Or just click the arrow next to **GO TO** and the books of the Bible will appear in a drop-down menu. Select the book you want and the chapter numbers will drop

A COURSE OF A DIFFERENT COLOR
You can always tell which section of *iLumina* you're in by the color scheme.
* The Bible: navy blue
* Encyclopedia: red
* Time Travel: gold
* Media Center: purple
* My Study Center: green
* Extras: black

down. When you release the mouse button, the Bible passage you selected will appear. Now you can select your preferred version in the space to the right.

You can use this **GO TO** feature from any screen in the Bible section of *iLumina*.

You can also use the large panel on the right side of the Bible Welcome screen (this panel is called the Bible Resource Index). If **BIBLE BOOKS** is highlighted in the adjoining tab, the 66 books of the Bible will be listed (in either alphabetical order or biblical order, it's up to you). Since the panel isn't large enough to show all 66 books at once, use the scroll bar at the right to scroll up or down to the book you want. When you click on one of these books, the introduction for that Bible book will appear. There *iLumina* provides a wealth of helpful background information about the book. Below the main text of the introduction, a clear **GO TO BIBLE BOOK** link will plunge you into chapter 1, verse 1.

TIP

IF YOU'RE FAIRLY NEW TO THE BIBLE, WHERE SHOULD YOU START READING?

Genesis is good—it will give you the beginnings of basically everything—and you can continue into Exodus, but after you reach the Ten Commandments (Exodus 20), you can skip ahead a bit. Sample the Psalms if you like; these expressions of prayer and praise are truly timeless. To learn about Jesus, go right to the Gospels: Matthew, Mark, Luke, or John. We suggest a New Testament reading plan of four books in a row—Luke (the basic Jesus story); John (same story, but with unique insights); Acts (the story of the first Christians); and Romans (what it all means).

VIEWING THE BIBLE TEXT

The Bible text appears in the center of the screen, with one chapter at a time available to you. Since most chapters of the Bible won't fit in the text area, you can move the text up and down *within that chapter* by using the scroll bar.

If you are viewing the New Living Translation, you will notice asterisks (*) in the text from time to time. These indicate that there is a special textual note for that verse (it would be a footnote in a printed Bible). If you click the word next to the asterisk, the footnote will appear in the Reference window on the lower left. These notes are usually about translation issues or cross-references.

The text area of the Bible screen is similar to a word processor, in that you can highlight text and use your mouse or keyboard to copy text to your computer's clipboard. (You can't type your own text in this area, but you *can* in My Study Center; see page 167).

If you select the **NLT & KJV SIDE-BY-SIDE** option, you can look at the same chapter in both the New Living Translation and King James Version. Both will scroll up or down together.

CHANGING THE SIZE OF THE BIBLE TEXT

See those three round buttons stacked at the lower right corner of the Bible text screen? Those can change the size of the

Bible text you're reading. The small T on the bottom makes it smaller. The big T in the middle makes the text larger. The page icon at the top is the **UNHIGHLIGHT TEXT** button, setting the text back to its original style. You can also use this if you have highlighted words in the text (from a previous search) that you now want to unhighlight.

PAGING THROUGH THE BIBLE

Above the Bible text, you see a title bar. Like the sign hanging at a railroad depot, this tells you where you are, with a verse listing and a title for your current section. That title might change as you scroll down to a different section within the same chapter. To flip to the *next chapter*, click the double arrow at the right of that sign (and pointing right). The arrow-line icon will take you to the *next book* of the Bible. The arrows at the left, pointing left, will flip back to the *previous chapter* or *book*.

But that "depot sign" hanging there—that does far more than just tell you where you are. It can help you browse through the text. We call it the **BLUEPRINT BROWSER**. In a

MY WORD!
When the makers of *iLumina* first envisioned this software—before all the animation and virtual reality came to be—they imagined a computer Bible you could take to church with you. So when the pastor said, "Turn to Ephesians 2:8," you could push a few buttons and do just that—and probably faster than most of those who were turning pages. *iLumina* has become so much more, but it could still be used in that way. Just load it up on your laptop and fire it up when you get to church. But no peeking at the animations while the pastor's preaching, ok?

⊕ *By using the buttons in the lower right corner of the screen, you can make the Bible text appear in large print.*

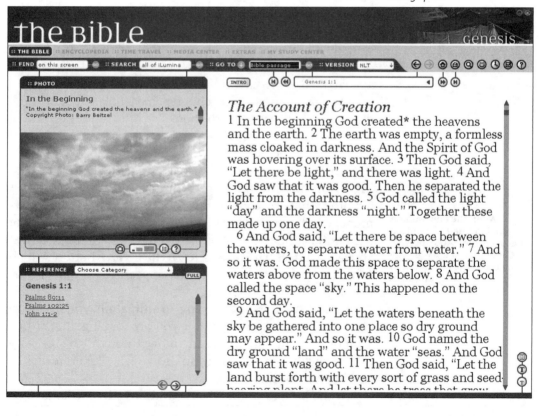

printed Bible, you might flip through page after page of the Gospel of John, looking for "The Feeding of the 5,000." You know it's there somewhere, but what chapter? Many modern Bibles have section headings that will speed your search—you just scan these titles until you hit pay dirt. The **BLUEPRINT BROWSER** lets you do the same thing, only faster. Click on the Scripture reference at the left of that title bar. You'll see the section-by-section outline of that book appearing in front of you. Find the section you want, click on it, and you'll go directly to that text.

VIEWING THE BIBLE: USING THE MEDIA WINDOW

As you look at the Bible text, you'll see two windows at the left. The upper one is the Media window, with several visual elements that can enhance your reading pleasure. You can learn far more about the various media options in the Media Center portion of this book (chapter 6), but for now you might need to know a few things about this window as you page through the Bible.

In *iLumina*, every Bible chapter has at least one media element that goes with it—usually a photo or a map, but occasionally it's an animation or one of the exciting Virtual Tours or Point in Time experiences. Whatever it is, that display will appear in the Media window automatically whenever you turn to that chapter. Some chapters have more than one media element associated with them.

Any item in the Media window can be adjusted in various ways. So it's useful to know your way around this window. At the top, the title bar tells you what kind of media you're looking at—if it's "Animation," that word lights up. If it's "Photo," that word lights up. Above the image, most elements will have a caption. Longer captions will make use of the scroll bar on the right, letting you read their full text. Just above the scroll bar is the **SHOW/HIDE TEXT** button, which will allow you to hide the caption appearing with an animation if you find it distracting.

If the display area is showing an animation, you'll need to click **PLAY** to bring it to life. If you are looking at a Virtual Tour or Point in Time, you can "move through" the scene by mouse-clicking and dragging on this screen. (For more on Virtual Tours, see chapter 6.)

At the bottom of the Media window is the Media toolbar,

with various controls depending on what kind of media is displayed. An animation will have all the controls available, so let's look at the one in Exodus 25 as an example. Once the Bible text appears, the first frame of the animation will appear in the Media window. Look at the Media toolbar. From the left, there's the **PLAY/PAUSE** button (to start an animation) and the **STOP** button (to stop it), as well as a **PROGRESS SLIDER** (to show how far in the animation you are) and a **VOLUME** button. You can drag the **PROGRESS SLIDER** at any time during the animation to take it to any portion of the animation you wish to view.

Next you'll see the camera icon*, which may become one of your favorite *iLumina* features. This is the **SNAPSHOT** button, allowing you to save an image of whatever you're viewing. Later, you can view the images you have snapped and use them in My Study Center*. You can snap anything in this media window—a frame of an animation, Virtual Tour, or Point in Time, as well as any map or photo. If you're looking at some great image, and you want to show it to your Sunday school class, well, you can. Just click that button. (For more on the Snapshot feature see chapter 8, My Study Center)

TIP

You can drag the dot on the Progress Indicator to move forward or back to a precise point in an animation.

⊕ *The Media window toward the upper left corner can hold maps, photos, or animations as it does here in Exodus 25.*

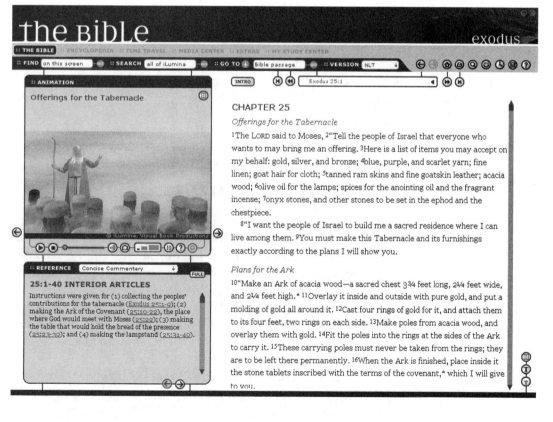

TIP

No need to pause the animation. Just click the SNAPSHOT as it goes, and you'll get a single-frame shot.

To the right of the **SNAPSHOT** button is the **SIZE SELECTOR**. You see three different sized blocks there: small, large, and theater-sized. If the Media window is too tiny for you (that's the "small" setting), click the medium setting. You'll be taken to the Media Center where the image will fill the center of the screen—that's the normal Media Center size. Clicking the largest block puts you in Theater Mode, where the image fills the entire screen. After viewing in the desired mode, click the **RETURN** button to get back to the Bible text (and put the image back in the Media window).

To the right of the **SIZE SELECTOR** is the **INDEX** button. Click here to get a list of all the visual elements of the current type that are available for that particular book of the Bible. So if you're in Ezekiel, looking at a photo of the Valley of Dry Bones, click here to find all the other photos keyed to Ezekiel. Beside that is the **HELP** button. At the far right of the Media toolbar, with some animations or Virtual Tours, is the **POINT IN TIME** button. When this is blinking, click on it to enter the biblical story. (More on this feature on page 96.)

DISCOVERING *ILUMINA*

Reaching Out with *iLumina*

For years, Anthony had been inviting Dan to church events. Dan had found a hundred ways to say no. Oh, he liked Anthony, but he had sworn off church as a teenager. Too many rules. Too many hypocrites.

Still Anthony kept asking—with a sincere enthusiasm that was wearing Dan down. If more Christians were real like Anthony, Dan thought, maybe the church wouldn't be so bad. But he still wouldn't chance it.

One evening, during their weekly bowling excursion, Anthony kept talking about this cool computer program he had just tried. Dan perked up, until he heard it was a Bible program.

"Honestly, Dan, I think even you would have fun with it," Anthony was saying. "Look, I'll bet you. If you try this out—actually read a book of the Bible—and if you don't like it, I'll stop bugging you about coming to church for three months."

"Three months? Make it six and you're on."

As they negotiated the wager further, it was decided that Dan would read the Gospel of Mark on the *iLumina* program over the next month. He was on his honor to really read it, not just skim it. And if he wanted to check out some of the additional features of the computer program, that was entirely optional.

The next day at work, Anthony came back from lunch carrying a new copy of *iLumina*. "Here you go, buddy. Call me if you need any help with it."

Dan was curious about how the program was put together, so he installed it that night and started playing with it. He quickly decided that the Encyclopedia had little that he would be interested in. As far as he was concerned, if there was any word in the English language that rivaled *Bible* in sheer boredom, it was *Encyclopedia*. He shuddered to think how dull a *Bible Encyclopedia* would be.

The Time Travel section, however, was kind of interesting. Seeing the spread of history like that was helpful, even if he didn't care about half of those events. He liked grabbing the timeline and pulling it back and forth to bring a new century into view.

Dan looked at the real time and decided he'd better go ahead and start reading the Bible. Bypassing the other sections of *iLumina,* he went to the Bible section, found Mark in the Bible reference menu, and saw the introduction to that book appear before him.

Too much information! A map, a timeline, an introduction, facts about the book. *This would be great if I really cared about all this*, he thought. *But I just want to get this over with.* He quickly clicked the **GO TO BIBLE BOOK** command and was staring at Mark 1:1. "Here begins the Good News about Jesus the Messiah . . . "

Good news, he thought. *Well, I could use some of that.* And he continued to read. The language was clear and the stories were interesting. Jesus was getting baptized. Jesus was healing people. Some people followed him. Some opposed him.

Dan had intended to read only the first chapter, but he was captivated by the story. He clicked to chapter 2 and read on. Then chapter 3. Suddenly the Media window, which had been graced by photos of ancient sites, had a cartoon in it. Not anything goofy, but an animated picture of a man at a podium in some kind of meeting room. He clicked on the image and it came to life. It was Jesus in a synagogue, healing a man's shriveled hand.

He got about halfway through Mark that night, and came back the next night to finish it up. Then he started reading Luke.

CHAPTER THREE

⊖ STUDYING THE BIBLE

USING THE REFERENCE WINDOW

Many Bible readers like to have extra resources close at hand—commentary, study notes, discussion questions, or devotional thoughts. Bookstore shelves overflow with Bibles that carry these various helps. *iLumina* gives you all of that in one product. The reference material shows up in the Reference window at the bottom left of the Bible text screen.

Cross-references will automatically appear there, keyed to whatever Bible text you're reading. But you can also choose from several other Bible Companions to illuminate the text as you read. If you click on the down-arrow next to Life Application Notes at the top of the Reference window, a drop-down menu will list the resources available. Click on any of those, and you'll see that reference in this window, keyed to your current Bible text. (For more information on the Bible Companions, see page 20.)

Use the scroll bar, if necessary, to see the entire text of the notes. The arrows at the bottom right of the Reference window will take you to the notes for the *next Bible verse* or the *previous Bible verse* (or at least the next or previous notes *available* in that particular Bible Companion). The **FULL** button at the upper right enlarges the notes, taking you to the Bible Companions screen.

RESEARCHING WORDS OR VERSES IN THE BIBLE

While reading the Bible text, you can right-click on any word (Control-click on a Mac) and *iLumina*'s Context menu will pop up on your screen near your mouse pointer. This menu is your gateway to thousands of Bible Companion articles, Encyclopedia articles, prayers*, study notes, and much more.

TIP

You can drag the cursor to highlight text *within* the Reference window and copy it to My Study Center*, or your own documents.

Within this Context menu, you can choose to **ADD TO FAVORITES** or **COPY** the selected text, or you can select **LOOK UP WORD** to find a definition in *iLumina*'s English Language Dictionary. Another option is to **SEARCH WORD,** which will scour *iLumina* for all other occurrences of the word you clicked on.

The Context menu also has five Resource Categories:

- Bible Notes
- Commentaries
- Cross-References
- Devotional Resources
- Study Resources

SECRET

Look up Psalm 145:7 (NLT) and read about sharing God's story. Then ALT-click on the "Psalms" title at the very top right of the screen to see how the animated stories in *iLumina* got started.

Each of these resource categories can contain multiple options (especially in *iLumina Gold*). For instance, when you point your mouse at **BIBLE NOTES**, a second menu appears with the **LIFE APPLICATION** and **PRAISE AND WORSHIP** options. Selecting either of these options will display those notes in the Reference window. When you click on **CROSS-REFERENCES**, a list of related verses will appear. Click one of them and it will appear in the Reference window. Clicking on any of those references will take you directly to that text.

USING CHARTS AND BIBLE STUDIES

If you are teaching a Bible class, leading a small group Bible study, or just getting serious about learning Scripture on your own, you might want to tap into *iLumina*'s supply of charts and Bible study guides. There are hundreds of them, for many different portions of Scripture.

Say you're already reading a Bible text, and you wonder, *Hmmm, is there a chart or Bible study on this passage?* Then right-click on a verse, highlight **STUDY RESOURCES**, and see if **CHARTS** or **BIBLE STUDIES** appears on the submenu. If so, click it.

But if you're just starting your study, click on **THE BIBLE** in the menu bar up top. Then, in the Bible Welcome screen, look under Bible Companions, under Study Resources and click on **CHARTS** or **BIBLE STUDIES**. That will take you to the Charts and Bible Studies screen.

Then something new happens—you might have to wait a few seconds as *iLumina* actually loads another program into itself—you'll be looking at an *iLumina* screen, but the Viewer window on the right will be running the Adobe Reader program, which will display your chart or study guide. There's a good reason for that, which we'll get to on page 114.

Please note that the normal *iLumina* commands and functions will not work within that window. Adobe Reader has its own toolbar at the top of that window. From here you can print out the chart or study you want. Use the print command in the Adobe Reader's toolbar to do that. It's the second icon from the left at the top of the viewer window. (You have permission to make up to 50 copies for use in nonprofit, noncommercial settings—like a church Bible study group.) To learn more about using Adobe Reader's functions see page 114.

Use the Index window on the left to select any other charts or Bible studies you might need. Click on the plus sign beside a Bible book to see all charts and studies available for that book. Click on the title bar at the top of the Index window to access other types of resource material.

TIP

It's difficult to edit charts and studies, but not impossible. Here's how.

1. With Adobe's toolbar (see page 114), select the sections you want to use and click the COPY button (or CTRL+C).

2. Minimize *iLumina* with the button at the uppermost right.

3. Start your own word-processing program.

4. Place your cursor on that page and click PASTE (or CTRL+V). The copied text will appear there.

5. Now you can work with that text in your word processor as much as you'd like.

⊕ *Right-click on any word in the Bible text and the Bible context menu will appear.*

Bible Companions

Here's the breakdown of the Bible Companions available through the Context menu:

BIBLE NOTES
- Life Application (from the *Life Application Study Bible*)
- Praise and Worship (from the *Praise and Worship Study Bible*)

COMMENTARIES
- Comprehensive (from *The New Commentary on the Whole Bible*)
- Concise (from the *Tyndale Concise Bible Commentary*)
- Life Application (from the *Life Application Commentary* series, New Testament only)

CROSS-REFERENCES
- A list of related verses

DEVOTIONAL RESOURCES
- Devotions (from *One Year through the Bible*)
- Prayers (from *The Praise and Worship Study Bible*)
- Praise and Worship Profiles (from *The Praise and Worship Study Bible*)
- Reading Plan (from *The One Year Bible*)

STUDY RESOURCES
- Life Application Bible Studies
- Bible Charts
- Links to the Encyclopedia
- People Profiles (from the *Life Application Study Bible*)
- Small Group Discussion Questions

PICKING A BIBLE COMPANION

What if you want to focus on the helpful resources just mentioned, and not just on the Bible text? What if you want to see these resources in a fuller version, not crammed into a corner of the Bible screen? You can do that.

From the Bible text screen, click the **FULL** button at the top right of the Reference window. You will be taken to the Bible Companions screen, where the resources get the greatest attention, and the appropriate Scripture references have the smaller box.

From anywhere else in *iLumina*, click on **THE BIBLE** in the menu bar. (Or at startup, just click on **THE BIBLE** in the opening screen.) That gets you to the Bible Welcome screen where, in the second column from the left, is the heading Bible Companions. Click on one of the resources listed, and you'll be transported to the wonderful world of Bible Companions.

If you want background information on the *whole* Bible, or an introduction to any of the books of the Bible, look under Bible Overview.

USING THE BIBLE COMPANIONS

Let's review.

What are Bible Companions? A collection of notes and resources keyed to the Bible text. Look back at page 20 for the list of resources.

You can access notes from these resources by right-clicking a word or verse in the Bible text, or by looking at the comments in the Reference Window. But to do your most serious research, you'll want to get to the big screen.

How can you get to the Bible Companions screen? The easiest way is to click **THE BIBLE** in the menu bar up top and choose a specific Bible Companion from the drop-down menu. Or, if

⊕ *Clicking the Full button in the Reference window moves the reference material to center screen.*

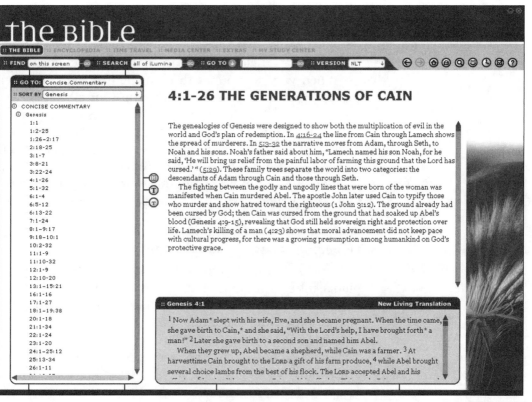

you're already reading the Bible text, click **FULL** in the Reference window.

Once in this screen, you'll see the Bible Companion content, front and center. You'll see the notes from the resource you selected, keyed to the Bible text you were just working on (or, if you're just starting out, default content is shown, usually keyed to Genesis 1:1). You can scroll through the notes or the Scripture. That's easy enough. And remember those three text bubbles can change the size of the text you're reading (see page 10).

But the really cool stuff in this screen happens in the panel on the left—we call it the Companions Index window. (Obviously, all the really good names were taken.) Here's where you can browse through thousands of possible articles to find just what you want.

Start by clicking where it says **GO TO** at the top of this window. That will unfurl a menu of resources available. Click on one you like, and the index for that resource will appear in the window. Most of these are indexed by books of the Bible, but some have alphabetical lists of articles. Use the scroll bar at the right of the window to move down through the index until you find what you want. If you're looking for material on a particular Bible reference, click on the plus sign next to the Bible book. That should produce a sub-outline of chapters, verses, or articles. Just zero in on the reference you want.

When you click on a listing in the Companions Index window, that article should appear in the central screen area.

If you're looking for material on a certain subject, you can type a topic in the **FIND** text box and click **GO**. This will yield a list of all article titles *within the current resource* that include your target word. Note: The search function only looks through titles at this point, not the text of those articles. For a more comprehensive search, see page 64.

USING THE BIBLE OVERVIEW

Say you're starting a study of the book of Acts. Before you plunge into the analysis of Acts 1:1, you want to get the overview of the book. Who wrote it? When did these things happen? What are the major themes?

The Bible Overview screen will help you do that. The easiest way to get here, from anywhere in *iLumina*, is to click **THE BIBLE** in the menu bar at the top and select **BIBLE OVERVIEW** from the drop-down menu.

As with the Companions, the main text appears in the center, but you'll do most of your work in the left-side panel, the Overview Index window. Click on the title bar at the top of that window to reveal three resources you can choose from—**BIBLE BOOK OVERVIEWS**, **VERSION INTRODUCTIONS**, and **QUESTIONS ABOUT THE BIBLE**.

You want to know about Acts, so click on **BIBLE BOOK OVERVIEWS**. You'll see that familiar list of Bible books appearing. Scroll down to find Acts and click on the plus sign next to it.

Now you have five more choices, introductory info from five different resources.

- **IN BRIEF:** short book description, list of themes
- **CONCISE INTRODUCTION:** to-the-point comments focusing on the whole book
- **COMMENTARY INTRODUCTION:** background information and connection to other books

⊕ *The Bible Overviews are the quickest way to learn about the people, history, and themes of the different books of the Bible.*

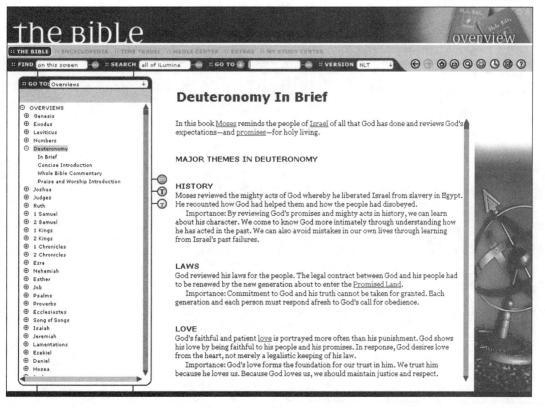

- **PRAISE AND WORSHIP INTRODUCTION:** worship-related themes and applications
- **APPLICATION INTRODUCTION** (NT only): how to get the Scripture into your life

Click on the one that seems most interesting to you, and that text will appear in the center of the screen.

If you're doing a study of Bible translations, you might want to learn more about a Bible version as a whole. Go back to the title bar (of the Overview Index window) and click **VERSION INTRODUCTIONS**. In *iLumina*, you can read the introduction to the New Living Translation. *iLumina Gold* also gives you the introductory dedication from the King James Version. Future editions of *iLumina* will include even more translations.

Now let's look at the third option. Go back to the title bar and click **QUESTIONS ABOUT THE BIBLE**. You'll see a cascade of questions commonly asked about Scripture. Click on one that interests you, and see the answer in the center of the screen.

For more detailed explanations of the various screens available in the Bible section of *iLumina*, see pages 87–115.

SECRET

Look up Acts 17:28 (NLT) to see how we live and even "move" in the Lord. Then ALT-click on the "Acts" title at the very top right of the screen; you'll go to a place where *iLumina* really gets moving.

CHAPTER FOUR

USING THE ENCYCLOPEDIA

IN ORDER TO GRAB the Encyclopedia and look up topics, start by clicking on **ENCYCLOPEDIA** on the *iLumina* Home Page.

OR, you can also get to the Encyclopedia from any other screen by clicking on **ENCYCLOPEDIA** in the menu bar.

And before your eyes, the Encyclopedia Welcome screen will be inviting you to "Explore. Discover. Learn. Begin." This is your avenue to nearly 9,000 articles on subjects from the Bible and Christian experience.

But *iLumina* has more than sheer numbers. Remember: this product is all about the visual, the interactive, the practical. So the Encyclopedia has different kinds of articles for different uses. A number of the articles have pictures for your viewing pleasure; some will make you laugh, and some will even sing to you.

8,900 ARTICLES!
If you looked up one article in this Encyclopedia every hour, it would take you a year to get through it. (Don't try that, though. You need your sleep.)

SELECTING A FOCUS AREA
IN THE ENCYCLOPEDIA

Yes, I know you're eager to start searching, but you will save time later if you take a minute now to consider the focus areas of this Encyclopedia.

iLumina Gold has seven focus areas (*iLumina* has four). If you already know the sort of information you're looking for, you can narrow your search to a single focus area. Just click on the picture or title of your chosen focus area. An alphabetical index will appear. You can immediately scroll to the exact subject you're looking for, or just browse through the index.

If you want to sift through the entire Encyclopedia, click on **ALL ARTICLES**.

The following focus areas are available:

TIP

If you click on ALL ARTICLES, you'll need to wait a minute for the program to gather all the different indexes. Why not enjoy a refreshing beverage?

TOP TOPICS

More than 100 crucial subjects are given the royal treatment, with pictures, maps, fun stuff, and sometimes animations or Virtual Tours. If you're looking for information on major topics or broad subjects like Abraham, Assyria, or Archaeology, start here. Or you might want to browse here for ideas for a lesson to teach or a paper to write.

BIBLE DICTIONARY
With over 5,000 articles, the Bible Dictionary is your one-stop resource for information about virtually any topic related to the Bible. There are articles about every person, place, and event in the Bible. There are articles about every book of the Bible. There are even articles about every plant and animal mentioned in the Bible. If it's in the Bible and you need to know more about it—look here.

LIFE APPLICATION
Have questions about major topics of the Christian faith and life? The Life Application focus area contains nearly 1,000 articles designed to help you apply information about key biblical topics like salvation, justification, and repentance. There are also articles designed to help you with life issues like abortion, alcohol and drug use, divorce, and much more.

CHRISTIAN HISTORY
If you're looking for information on Christians who have lived since Bible times, this is the place to go. Augustine, Francis of Assisi, Martin Luther, John Calvin, and Billy Graham are all here, along with about 1,500 of their close personal friends.

DEUTERO-CANONICAL BOOKS*
There's a collection of about 15 books commonly known as the Apocrypha and sometimes included in Bibles between the Old and New Testaments. The Roman Catholic church views these as part of sacred Scripture; Protestant denominations don't. Whatever your perspective, they are relevant ancient works that will help you understand Jewish history and culture, so *iLumina* includes them here for you to study. Click on any of the book titles to read it, or search for your target theme within its text.

HYMNS*
Music has long been an integral part of Christian worship. Through the centuries, believers have written hymns that have expressed both the content of Christian faith and their

feelings about it. In this focus area of *iLumina*, you'll find the lyrics of several hundred traditional hymns, along with devotional text to help you gain a better understanding of what the hymn means, who wrote it, and how it can help you gain a richer understanding of God and his Word. Selected hymns even have an audio rendition of the melody, so you can hear what the hymn sounds like.

THEOLOGY*

Throughout the history of the church and its study of Scripture, many ideas have developed about who God is and how he works. If you're wondering about predestination, omnipotence, or transubstantiation, you might not find those terms in the Bible itself, but you can learn about them in the Theology focus area. Relax—there are shorter words there too, like *grace* and *faith*. This Focus Area includes definitions of key terms, Scripture passages that are frequently quoted, and biblical topics that every Christian should know about.

Once you select your Focus Area, the Encyclopedia will open for you. The index of your chosen Focus Area (or the en-

⊕ *The Encyclopedia's focus areas are listed under Encyclopedia on the menu bar.*

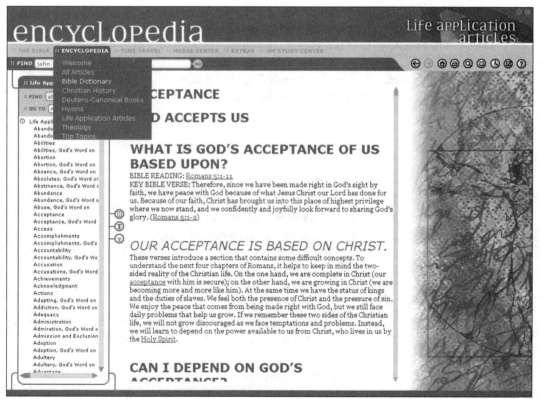

tire Encyclopedia if you chose **ALL ARTICLES**) will appear in the Index window.

USING THE SEARCH BAR

It will be tempting to type your topic in the space in the Search bar, but that might not be the best thing to do. That will search *all* of *iLumina* for your subject, which is great if you want an exhaustive list of every mention. But first you probably just want to read the main Encyclopedia entry. So click on the proper Focus Area (or **ALL ARTICLES**) and use the **FIND** function in the Article Index window to zero in on your article.

USING THE FIND FUNCTION

Once you select a focus area, the Encyclopedia Entry screen will appear. At this point, you want to look at the Index window on the left. You could scroll down to the article you want, but it's faster to type your target topic in the **FIND** space at the top. Then you'll be whisked right to the listing for the article you want. Then click on that, and the article will appear in the main text area.

We're assuming that there is an entry for your topic in that focus area. Actually, the **FIND** function will list all article titles containing the word or phrase you typed. If you type "John" in the **FIND** space for Bible Dictionary Index, it will list John, John the Baptist, and at least four books of the Bible bearing that name.

What should you do if the **FIND** function finds nothing?

1. **CHECK YOUR SPELLING.** The **FIND** function will look for exactly what you typed.
2. **TRY A SYNONYM OR RELATED TOPIC.** You might not find *wickedness*, but you will find *evil*.
3. **CHOOSE A DIFFERENT FOCUS AREA.** St. Augustine is old, but not *that* old. You won't find him in the Bible Dictionary, but you will in the Christian History focus area. Click on the title bar at the top of the Index window. That should give you a menu of the available focus areas. Click on a new one and then retype your query in the **FIND** space.
4. **USE THE SEARCH BAR.** If you've tried 1-3 and still find nothing, move to the **SEARCH** text box and type your

TIP

Longer indexes are divided by letter. It's something like one of those big dictionaries with letter tabs. Click the letter to the right of GO TO which hangs below the title bar to the left, and select the first letter of the topic you're looking up. Then scroll down to the right article.

topic there. That will take a minute, but the program should yield a list of every occurrence of your word or phrase anywhere it appears in *iLumina*—within Scripture, within any article of the Encyclopedia, and within any media caption.

VIEWING ENCYCLOPEDIA ENTRIES

In the center of the Encyclopedia Entry screen, you see the main article you've chosen. Use the scroll bar, if necessary, to move up or down.

Any words highlighted in the text (a different color) can link you to other Encyclopedia articles on those subjects. Just click on them.

Any highlighted Bible reference can link you to that text in the Bible section of *iLumina*. Just click on it.

You can also get a definition of any word from *iLumina*'s English dictionary. Just right-click on that word. (Control-click for Mac).

Just like the Bible text, Encyclopedia text can be selected

Every article in the *iLumina* Encyclopedia belongs to only one *focus area*. If you see an article in one focus area index that has the same name as an article in another, the content of the articles is different.

⊕ *Typing a word or phrase such as "John of" into the Find box will show you all the articles with those words in the title for your selected focus area.*

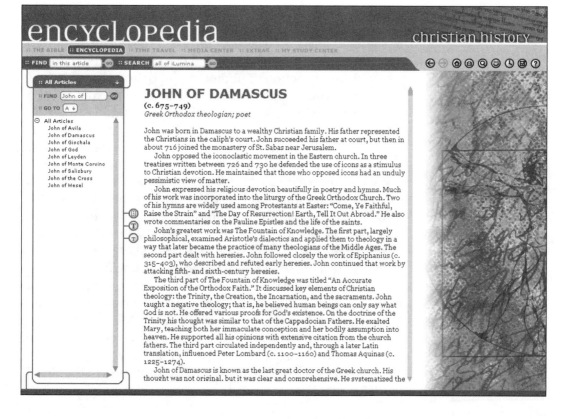

and copied to your computer's clipboard. This will be valuable to you as you use My Study Center (see page 72).

The size of the text can also be altered by using the round buttons at the left of the article. (Large T makes it larger, small T smaller, and the icon above these restores it to its original size.)

Many Encyclopedia entries include some sort of media, usually a picture, which will appear automatically in the Media window at the right. Some entries include both a Media window and a Reference window at the bottom right. Hymn entries include a Hymn window with the words of the song. A number of entries, especially the shorter ones, have just the main text, with no special windows appearing at the right.

VIEWING THE MEDIA WINDOW

If an Encyclopedia entry has more than one visual element available, one will be displayed in the main Media window, and you'll be able to use the right and left arrows on either side of the Media toolbar to see the others. You can use the Media Chooser bar at the top of the Media window to pick the type of image you want to see—Animations, Photos, Maps, or Virtual Tours.

Below the thumbnails you'll find a title and caption for the main image. The **INDEX** button (the page icon to the right of the title) will take you back to the Media Center to look at the entire collection of photos, maps, or animations.

If the display area is showing an animation, you'll need to click on it to bring it to life. Clicking on a running animation will pause it until you click again. If you are looking at a Virtual Tour or Point in Time, you can "move through" the scene by dragging your mouse on this screen. (For more on those activities, see page 41.)

At the bottom of the Media window is the Media toolbar, with various controls pertaining to various kinds of media. For the animations, you have the **PLAY/PAUSE** button and the **STOP** button, as well as a **PROGRESS SLIDER** (to show how far in the animation you are) and a **VOLUME** button.

The **SNAPSHOT** button (the camera) allows you to save an image of whatever you're viewing. Later, you can view the images you have snapped and use them in My Study Center*. You can snap anything in this media window—a frame of an animation or Virtual Tour, as well as any map or photo.

To the right of the **SNAPSHOT** button is the **SIZE SELECTOR**. Three sizes are available to you. The Media window itself is the smallest size. Clicking on the medium size will take you to the Media Center, where it will fill the center of the screen. Clicking the large size puts you in Theater Mode, where the image fills the entire screen. After viewing in the desired mode, click the **RETURN** button to get back to the Bible text (and put the image back in the Media window).

To the right of the **SIZE SELECTOR** is the **HELP** button, and at the far right of the Media toolbar, the **POINT IN TIME** button will appear with some animations or Virtual Tours. When this is blinking, click on it to enter the biblical story. (More on this feature on page 96.)

VIEWING THE REFERENCE WINDOW

Each of the articles in the Top Topics focus area has a Reference window with a six-course feast of menu items available.

The Fast Facts appear first, displaying the various sections of these articles. So if you're researching the reign of David as king, you don't have to wade through all that boring giant-

⊕ *Top Topics articles contain media content and features like Fast Facts to the right of the article.*

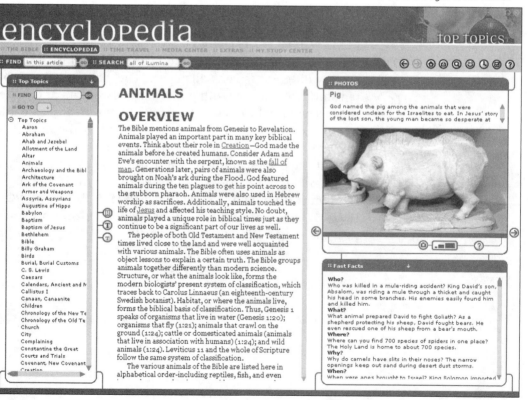

killing stuff. Scroll the outline to "David the King" and it will take you to that place in the article.

To see other reference material, click on the title bar and see the menu. You can choose from the following items:

- **FAST FACTS:** the who, what, when, where, and why of your subject in one glance.
- **WACKY WIT:** some creative angle on the subject. Although it's not always wacky, there's generally some wit involved.
- **DIGGING DEEPER:** Encyclopedia links to related subjects. Click on any of these to look up those related articles.
- **LIFE LINKS:** More links, but with a "life application" angle (for example: David's an example of living by faith. Click on "Faith" to find out more).
- **PEOPLE PROFILES:** Links to people who are related to your subject. If you're studying David, you might want to look up Jesse, Samuel, Goliath, Nathan, or Bathsheba as well. Click on their names in this list to go to those articles.

LISTENING TO HYMNS

If you've chosen to look something up in the Hymn section, a slightly different screen will appear. The main articles are often stories about the writing of a particular hymn and sometimes devotional thoughts about the hymn. In any case, the hymn text will appear in a special window at the right. Use the scroll bar to move up and down through those lyrics.

But the coolest thing is that, with some hymns, *iLumina* will play the music for you, too. See the controls just above the hymn title—**PLAY**, **STOP**, **PROGRESS SLIDER**, and **VOLUME**? When those appear, click the **PLAY** arrow and you'll hear the music. Why not sing along?

TIP

Wouldn't this be a great thing for family devotions? Or even your own personal quiet time? Gather around the computer and let it accompany your songs of praise!

USING THE ENCYCLOPEDIA

A Youth Leader Explores Suffering

Chris had been leading the youth group for three years, and in that time the group had grown 2000 percent. Yes, attendance had mushroomed from just one kid to twenty. Sometimes Chris had a tough time juggling his day job (managing a convenience store), his night classes at the seminary, and the increasing number of youth activities, but somehow he got it all done. It was especially rewarding to see the growth of the youth group–and not just the numerical growth. These kids were coming to know Jesus personally, learning the Bible, and applying it to the issues of their lives. He started a Tuesday night group called Explorers for kids who wanted to dig deeper into Scripture and deal with the tough questions.

One Tuesday the kids asked a particularly tough question, and Chris promised that they'd tackle it the next week. *Why does God allow suffering?* Over the next week Chris spent his days and nights mulling over the question—and how to "explore" it with his kids. By Saturday afternoon, he was still clueless, but he had to work on a paper for seminary, so he sat at his desk and tried to focus.

He'd been using this new software called *iLumina* for some of the initial research on seminary projects. Suddenly he wondered if *iLumina* could help him with the upcoming Explorers discussion. So he typed "suffering" into the Search bar. After a few seconds he had a huge list of Bible verses and articles. The list was a bit overwhelming. He decided to start with the Encyclopedia article on suffering and follow any links he could.

The main article was packed with Bible verses: Romans 8, the book of Job, some of the Psalms. As he read, he began to formulate the theological background for their discussion. Certainly the Explorers would benefit from the central points of this article, but he wanted this to be a practical matter, too, so he kept looking. He found the subject of suffering was also listed in the Life Application Articles. This treatment focused on specific life questions—the very questions his kids were asking. *Why am I suffering? Doesn't God care about me?* And here were more Scripture references, along with a discussion of possible answers. He book marked this page in his Favorites file.

Chris also found a link to an animation of the story from John 9 where a blind man is healed by Jesus. Of course! The disciples wondered why the man was suffering from blindness, thinking that maybe his parents had caused it through their sin. Jesus explained that the man was blind so that God's glory could be revealed in him. It's one thing to read those words, and quite another to see the story happening.

Now Chris was well prepared for Tuesday night. He printed a handout from the Encyclopedia material, and he brought his laptop so the group could view the story of the blind man. As it turned out, they ran the animation several times, and then the kids discovered the Point in Time connection, which let them step into the scene between the blind man and Jesus. They moused around the scene, reading the captions that appeared, and gaining a deeper sense of the story's background.

It was one of their best sessions yet. The kids were excited about this biblical story, and they understood the question of suffering in a whole new way—through the blind man's newly healed eyes.

CHAPTER FIVE

➔ TRAVELING THROUGH TIME

IN ORDER to start your Time Traveling, click on **TIME TRAVEL** on the *iLumina* home page.

OR, you can also get to the Time Travel section from any other screen by clicking on **TIME TRAVEL** in the menu bar.

You will see 14 historical pictures arranged in a circle. Is this some new design motif for your computer room? It can be if you have the desire to make it so, but within *iLumina* it's the Welcome screen for the Time Travel section.

SELECTING A TIME TRAVEL ERA

Try this. Position your mouse pointer on the image at the top of the circle. Then move your mouse slowly around the circle. The caption in the center will change as you go. You see, each of those pictures represents one of 14 eras of human history. The dates of each era are listed along with the title we've given that era. As you move your mouse, you are going "in one era and out the other." When you reach an era you're interested in, click your mouse. *Presto!* Your screen displays the information on that era.

TIME TRAVEL ERAS

- **BEGINNINGS** (?-1876 B.C.): Creation through the Patriarchs.
- **SLAVERY TO SETTLEMENT** (1876-1375 B.C.): Out of Egypt, into Canaan.
- **JUDGES AND KINGS** (1375-930 B.C.): Samson, Samuel, Solomon, and others.
- **THE DIVIDED KINGDOM** (930-586 B.C.): Division to destruction.
- **EXILE, RETURN, AND INDEPENDENCE** (586-6 B.C.): Jewish history from Jeremiah to Jesus.

- **JESUS' LIFE AND MINISTRY** (6 B.C. to A.D. 30): From Jesus' birth to his death, and beyond.
- **THE EARLIEST CHURCH** (A.D. 30-100): Pentecost to Patmos.
- **THE CHURCH IN THE PAGAN ROMAN EMPIRE** (100-312): Growth despite persecution.
- **THE AGE OF THE CHRISTIAN ROMAN EMPIRE** (312-800): Constantine to Charlemagne.
- **THE HOLY ROMAN EMPIRE** (800-1517): The Middle Ages.
- **THE REFORMATION** (1517-1648): Luther's revolution and radical change.
- **THE AGE OF REASON AND REVIVAL** (1648-1789): Bunyan and Bach to Whitefield and Wesley.
- **AN ERA OF MISSIONS AND DENOMINATIONS** (1789-1914): Carey, Judson, Spurgeon, Moody.
- **A TIME OF CONFLICT AND TECHNOLOGY** (1914 to the present): Ups and downs of the recent century.

SECRET

You can actually slide from one era to the next. Click on the timeline and drag it forward or back, to reveal some of the events in the adjacent era.

Once you're in a particular era, you can move to any other era by simply clicking along the master timeline just under the era title. Or click the arrows at either end of that timeline to go forward or back one era.

WORKING WITH THE TIME TRAVEL SCREEN

For each chunk of history, we've presented some of its most important events. These are described briefly above and below the Era Timeline running across the center of the screen. The main purpose of this timeline is to give you a sense of what happened when. To find out more about any of the events, click on the highlighted words or names. That will take you to the corresponding article in the Encyclopedia.

Click on any Bible reference to look it up in the Bible section.

Some of the events listed have photos accompanying them. This means there's more information available in the Spotlight section at the right. Click on any picture to change the Spotlight contents.

Some of the events are accompanied by frames of animation. This means there's an animated story available in the Media Center on that subject. Click on the frame to go to the Media Center and automatically load up that animation.

USING THE SPOTLIGHT

The Spotlight panel at the right is a timeline-within-a-timeline. The main timeline covers about 5,000 years in 15 eras, listing fewer than 200 events. There's not much space available for the significant events *within* the lives of Abraham, Moses, David, or Jesus. But those are important too. The Spotlight allows us to take a magnifying glass to one part of the timeline, to see the developments in the lives of the major players in the Bible and Christian history.

Scroll down through the Spotlight panel as needed, to see all these life events. Remember you can change the subject of the Spotlight by clicking on one of the other photos in the main timeline area.

TIP

In the timeline, photos are square. They change the Spotlight content in the right panel. Animation frames are rectangular. They link to animations in the Media Center.

USING THE OTHER HAPPENINGS WINDOW

In the time of Moses, what was going on elsewhere in the world? What were the technological advances that affected David's battle plans? What world powers was Xerxes contending with when he wasn't dining with Esther? Who was

⊕ *The Other Happenings window is just below the time line and contains concise information to give you a broader picture of the era you're looking at.*

You can always tell immediately where you are in history by looking at the bold segment on the Master Timeline at the top, just under the era title. You can reposition that segment anywhere along the Master Timeline by clicking the timeline or clicking and dragging the segment with the mouse.

CAUGHT IN THE MIDDLE?

You might be asking, "What if I drag the timeline so that I'm half in one era and half in another? What title could possibly be displayed at the top of the screen?" A bit obsessive, are we? Well, our fabulous programmers have thought of that. In their excessive brilliance, they have determined that the screen content will snap to whichever era takes up most of the screen.

writing the best-sellers in Paul's day? What were the dominant world religions when Constantine became a Christian?

This is the sort of stuff you can find out in the Other Happenings window at the bottom of the Timeline screen. Six different categories of information have been culled for each of the fifteen eras. Click on one of the six subjects listed toward the left of that strip, and read the report at the right. Scroll down as needed.

The Other Happenings Categories

- **Technology:** What were the latest inventions affecting daily life, commerce, agriculture, or war?

- **World Power:** What nations were strongest? Who was battling whom?

- **Culture:** What were the customs of everyday life? What do we know about the art, music, and festivals of the time?

- **Religion & Philosophy:** Who was writing what about God, humanity, and the meaning of life?

- **Beyond the Middle East/Beyond the West:** In Bible history, the main attention is on the Middle East. So, what was going on elsewhere? In later Christian history, the focus shifts to Europe and then America. What was going on "beyond the West"?

CHAPTER SIX

 # EXPERIENCING THE MEDIA CENTER

TO ENTER the Media Center, click on **MEDIA CENTER** on the *iLumina* home page.

OR, you can also get to the Media Center from any other screen by clicking on **MEDIA CENTER** in the menu bar.

You will see six pictures, representing the six main areas of the Media Center: **ANIMATIONS, VIRTUAL TOURS, POINTS IN TIME, PHOTOS, BIBLE ATLAS,** and **GUIDED VIRTUAL TOURS.**

SELECTING YOUR CONTENT

Once you've selected your medium, you'll see a sample of that format in the center of your screen. At the left, a list of content for that medium will appear in the Index window. Some will be listed in alphabetical order, and others in Bible book order. Scan the Index window for the subject you want to see and click on it.

Note: if you ever want to switch media—say, move from photos to animations—just click on the title bar at the top of the Index window. Then, from the drop-down menu, choose the new medium you want.

VIEWING BIBLE ANIMATIONS

Once you've selected a particular animation, it begins playing in the center of your screen. Use the Media bar underneath the picture to control the animation. Left to right, you have the:

TIP

Whenever you see a plus sign next to an index entry, it means there are sub-entries under it. Click on the plus sign to see what's hidden.

 PLAY/PAUSE BUTTON: click here to start it, or if it's already running, this will pause the action.

 STOP BUTTON: this stops the action and resets to the beginning.

PROGRESS SLIDER: shows how far along in the animation you are; you can drag this to any point you want.

 VOLUME CONTROL: you can set the volume anywhere from "0" to "10" in the dialog box that appears when you click this.

SNAPSHOT BUTTON: click the camera icon to snap any frame of the animation (even if it's running) and save it for future use.

 SIZE SELECTOR: clicking this rectangle will put you in Theater Mode, where the animation nearly fills your computer screen.

HELP BUTTON: for any questions you might have.

 POINT IN TIME DIAMOND: occasionally this will flash during an animation. When it does, you can click it to freeze the action and enter the scene as a Point in Time. (See page 54 for more on Points in Time.)

SECRET

Take the Guided Virtual Tour to Nazareth, but then wander through that village on your own. Get to the carpenter's shop and enter it. You'll see an old wooden plow leaning against the door. Click on it and you'll see that our brilliant guides sometimes get plowed under.

All animations are Bible stories, with narration and dialogue taken straight from the Bible text (NLT). You can read along with the animation in the caption space underneath the picture.

TAKING VIRTUAL TOURS
SELECTING A TOUR

TIP

The animation begins playing as soon as you select it in the Index. If you're not quite ready, click the STOP button to reset it. It will resume when you click the PLAY button.

If you've selected **VIRTUAL TOURS** in the Media Center Welcome screen, you will see a biblical setting in the center of your screen. At first, the screen will begin to rotate slowly, but once you click it you will control what direction you face with the mouse. In the Index window at the left, you have your choice of several tours you could take. Click on the plus sign in front of the tour name to see the various "stops" available on any tour. Click on any of these to start your tour at that point.

Let's say you want to tour Jerusalem. You could start at the Pool of Siloam, the Synagogue, the Temple Mount, Herod's Palace, Golgotha, or several other places—take your pick. When you click on one of these sites, the center screen will change to that particular location. Now it's up to you to start moving through the city.

MOVING THROUGH THE TOUR

Oh, you thought this was going to be a bus tour? No such luck. You have to walk these streets, or at least you can mouse your computer through them.

The main skill you need in the Virtual Tour is the click-and-drag. Just click, and hold the clicker down as you slide the mouse right or left. The scene will change, as if you're turning your head right or left. Click and mouse forward— you're looking up. Click and mouse toward you—you're looking down. Play with this a bit to get the hang of it.

There's a caption below each scene, explaining what you're looking at, or what took place there. (In *iLumina Gold*, you also have the option of listening to a tour guide in certain places.) As you mouse around, the caption below the scene will change. So take your time and see all the different points of interest.

From any point in the tour you will see one or more bluish glass bubbles or spheres hovering at about eye level a short distance away. These are the stops on the Virtual Tour. Click one and you will move to that spot. There, you can mouse

Take the Guided Virtual Tour as far as Jesus' baptism in the Jordan River, but then look around the river on your own. You'll see a branch lying in the water. Click on it and you'll see what happens when our tour guides branch out on their own.

⊕ *The Virtual Tours allow you to walk through the temple and the streets of ancient Jerusalem.*

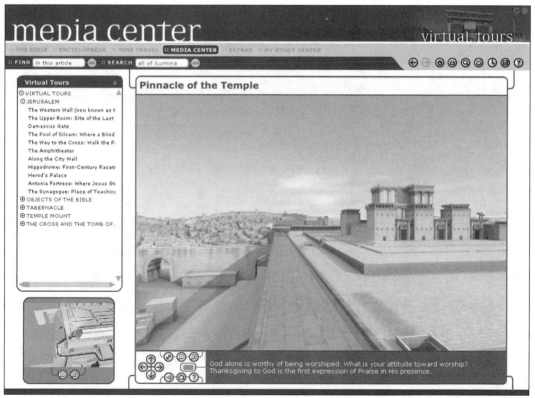

around and get different perspectives—or click forward to another new location.

GETTING YOUR BEARINGS WITH THE THUMBNAIL MAP

Sometimes you can get lost in a Virtual Tour. Don't worry. In the lower left-hand corner is a Thumbnail Map, showing you where you are in the larger scheme of things. Your position is a yellow dot. And the white triangle stemming from the yellow dot shows the direction you're looking. (Try moving the mouse side to side, and see how that triangle moves.) Green dots stand for any new positions you can move to. The blue line indicates the path through the tour, with blue dots showing other positions (the programmers call them nodes) along the way. The plus and minus arrows below the Thumbnail Map are your zoom controls. Get a closer look or a broader picture.

USING THE VIRTUAL TOOLBAR

This control bar has some different buttons from the other Media bars in *iLumina*. On the top row, you see:

 THE THUMBNAIL SWITCHER: that diagonal double arrow allows you to shift the Thumbnail Map from the corner to the main screen, switching places with the scene from the tour.

 ZOOM OUT: the minus magnifying glass zooms out, giving the impression of stepping backwards in the scene, getting a longer view.

 ZOOM IN: the plus magnifying glass zooms in, giving the impression of stepping forward.

On the bottom row are the familiar buttons:

 VOLUME CONTROL: choose a setting from 0-10 for the tour guide's voice and occasional music.

 SNAPSHOT: you can "snap a picture" of any Virtual Tour scene, saving it for My Study Center or another application.

 SIZE SELECTOR: as with the animations, you can do the Virtual Tours in Theater Mode, nearly filling your computer screen.

HELP BUTTON: just in case you're not getting all your questions answered by this book.

TAKING VIRTUAL TOURS OF BIBLE OBJECTS

You have the option of examining various Bible objects up close. These are mostly items in the tabernacle or temple, but a first-century fishing boat can also be viewed.

TIP

You can also zoom in and out on a Virtual Tour by using **SHIFT** (zoom in) and **CTRL** (zoom out) on your keyboard.

Once you click on a particular object to "take a tour" of, you will see that object in the center of your screen. The program is now displaying an "object movie" to give you a good look at the object you chose. It will stop whenever you click on the screen. Then you can turn the object by dragging it with your mouse.

Note: Most object tours do not have 360-degree range. But you can move the objects around somewhat, and look at them from above. Some also have automatic display features: the bread table will open as you turn it, revealing its trays; the ark of the covenant will open up as you look from above.

⊕ *The Thumbnail Switcher will allow you to view the Thumbnail Map up close to get an idea of where you are. Here Jerusalem is shown with the route of its Virtual Tour.*

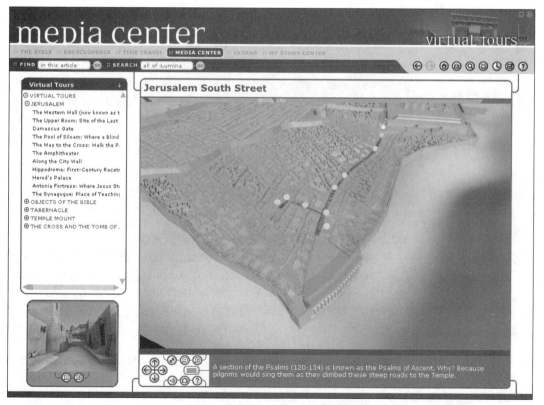

When "touring" an object, the click-and-drag doesn't move *you*, it moves the object. Think of it as if you're grabbing the object and turning it this way or that.

Programmer lingo: The different positions on the Virtual Tour (those dots on the Thumbnail map) are called *nodes*. The area on the screen where you can click to move on to the next node, we call a *hotspot*.

ENTERING POINTS IN TIME FROM A VIRTUAL TOUR

Every so often, you'll see a green diamond icon on a Virtual Tour. That's the sign for a Point in Time, which means that a biblical story happened in this very spot. If you click on the green diamond, you will suddenly be in the middle of that story, hearing a line from the story and seeing the people involved. And just as in the Virtual Tour, you can move around that scene. Click the diamond again to go back to the tour.

CHANGING TO A NEW TOUR

At any time, you can switch to a different Virtual Tour by going to the Index window at the left and clicking on a different entry. (Of course, you could also select a different position in your current tour. That is, if you're still stuck in South Jerusalem near the synagogue, and you want to get to the Upper Room without clicking your way through the streets, find it on the Index and click on it.)

CONNECTING TO A GUIDED VIRTUAL TOUR

Imagine yourself in a museum, sauntering from room to room on your own. But then you notice a group ahead of you, and a tour guide is saying some interesting things. You drift closer to hear, and when the group moves on, you tag along.

You have the same ability in *iLumina*'s Virtual Tours. Whenever you see that the large **PLAY** button to the lower left of the picture is not grayed out, you can click it to connect with a guided tour of Jesus' life and ministry. But be aware that this tour will automatically take you to its next site, so you might have to find your own way back (the **BACK** button should do that pretty easily). You can take the guided tour through as many sites as you want and leave it at any time.

TAKING GUIDED VIRTUAL TOURS

If you were to visit the Holy Land, you would probably want to connect with a guided tour to make sure you're seeing all the good stuff and getting the best information. It's the same way with the Virtual Tours of *iLumina*.

When you look at the Media Center Welcome screen, click **VIRTUAL TOURS** if you want to explore on your own. But if you want some help, click **GUIDED VIRTUAL TOURS**. Even if you're a bit of a lone ranger, you should check out at least

some of this guided tour.

After you click **GUIDED VIRTUAL TOURS** you'll see a map of Israel centered on your screen with a list of its regions in the left panel. As you mouse over any region listed, it will be highlighted on the map. Click on a region, and it will unfurl a list of sites within that region as the map flies you into that particular region. Now as you mouse over any site in the index, its location on the map will be highlighted.

Then click on a particular site in the index and you'll be transported to it. You can explore this on your own if you like—but then that wouldn't be a *guided* tour, now, would it? To find your guide, click the large **PLAY** button at the left end of the toolbar below the picture.

The guide will show you around that site, maybe the ancient site or maybe the same site in modern times. Then the guide will take you to another site and drop you off there. Check the map to see where you are. Here you can move around on your own again, or you can reconnect with the guide by clicking the large **PLAY** button. In that case, the guide will show you around, explain brilliant things, and then transport you to the next site on the tour. At each new

⊕ *Guided Virtual Tours not only provide you with video clips of sites in the Holy Land, but also with insights from experts in biblical history and archaeology.*

TIP

○

KEEP LOOKING DOWN
As you stroll through a Virtual Tour (including the Guided Tours), keep looking down. At certain locations you'll see a sphere at your feet. A golden or yellow sphere indicates that you can connect to a matching VR, racing through time to see the same site 20 centuries earlier or later. A green sphere means you can connect with a Point in Time, exploring a frozen moment of an actual biblical story. Just drag downward and, if you see a green or golden sphere, click it to go to that feature.

TIP

○

In many of the moving images of *iLumina*, you'll see colored spheres with different icons inside. These are passageways from one type of image to another. Green diamonds take you to Points in Time. A film frame takes you to a Guided Virtual Tour.

site, you have the option of going off on your own if you like, but you can always come back and click that **PLAY** button—your guide will be there, ready to go.

The entire guided tour covers the life of Jesus, site by site, in 42 segments, and lasts a total of about two hours (each segment lasts three minutes on average). It starts in Bethlehem, goes to Nazareth, Galilee, and Jerusalem, ending at the Mount of Olives and Jesus' ascension. Of course you can start at any point you click on the index, and you can wander away whenever you want.

FROM THE FIRST CENTURY TO THE TWENTY-FIRST

You'll notice that some of the Virtual Reality scenes are made up of photos from the modern day and others are graphic depictions of ancient times. At some stops on the tour you'll see golden glass bubbles instead of blue ones. At those sites you can switch between modern and ancient views by clicking the gold button with the diamond in it on the ground. To return to the tour, look straight down and click.

Those golden buttons fire up some of the coolest graphic images you'll ever see. Watch as ruins return to their pristine state, or see buildings fall apart as twenty centuries are compressed into a few seconds.

A VIRTUAL TOUR TUTORIAL

The Virtual Tours are a bit complex, but they're well worth the effort. So we're offering this brief tutorial to get you started. You could skip this section and play with the controls on your own—just go exploring, but if you want a more thorough and systematic approach, follow this step-by-step guide.

1. GET TO THE OPENING SCREEN FOR VIRTUAL TOURS.
(A) Click on **MEDIA CENTER** on the menu bar or in the
    iLumina Welcome screen.
(B) Click on the Virtual Tours picture in the Media Center
    screen.
        There is a default starting point in the center of your
    screen now, but we won't use that for this tour.

2. SELECT YOUR STARTING POINT. (FOR THIS TOUR WE'LL START AT THE SYNAGOGUE IN JERUSALEM.)
(A) Go to the Index window on the left and click the plus
    sign next to **JERUSALEM**.

(B) Scan the drop-down list until you see **THE SYNAGOGUE: PLACE OF TEACHING.** Click on that.

Now you see the inside of a first-century synagogue in Jerusalem.

3. EXPLORE.

(A) Click anywhere on the screen and hold the clicker down while you slowly drag the mouse left or right. You will be looking around the room. (Don't go too fast, you might get dizzy.) In fact, you can make a full 360-degree turn in the room. See the door to the outside?

(B) Try dragging up to look at the ceiling. Then drag down to look at the floor. Not much to look at here, but it's cool that you can look.

(C) Don't forget to read the captions, or listen to them if you are using *iLumina Gold,* as you go.

(D) Now return to your original position, looking into the building with the door at your back. Now zoom in, using the plus control below the screen (or use the Shift

⊕ *Our Virtual Tour Tutorial starts here in a synagogue in Jerusalem.*

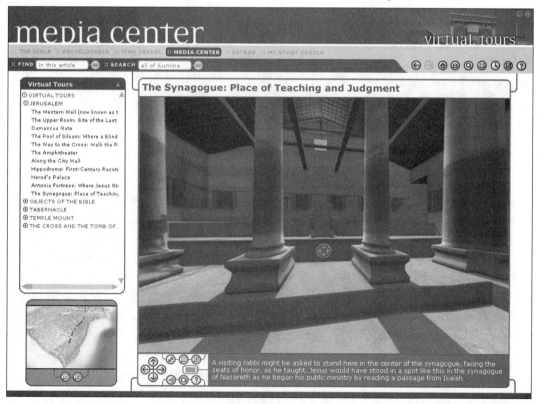

key). It will look as if you are walking into the room. Stop when you get about halfway in.

4. MOVE AHEAD.

(A) Simply click on the center of your screen. (Whenever the cursor looks like an up-arrow, or you see a blue bubble, you can click there to move to the position ahead of you.)

You have moved to the front of the synagogue, standing before the "seat of Moses." There's a green diamond there. That's the signpost for a Point in Time, your connection to a biblical scene that happened right here.

5. ENTER A POINT IN TIME AND LOOK AROUND.

(A) Click on the green diamond.

Suddenly there are people sitting in those chairs. Those are Pharisees, interrogating the blind man who had been healed by Jesus. You hear some words they say to him.

(B) Drag right, observing the entire scene.

See the formerly blind man making his case, and assorted other folks. (Jesus is not here at this time.)

You could poke around this scene, zooming in and out, looking up and down. You could also click on the animation link to see the Blind Man story, but right now we need to get back to the tour.

6. RETURN TO THE VIRTUAL TOUR.

(A) Click again on the button with the diamond.

You're back in an empty synagogue. Now it's time to go outside.

7. MOVE FORWARD TWO POSITIONS.

(A) Drag to rotate 180 degrees. Now you see the doorway.

(B) Click in the center of the screen. Now you're near the doorway.

(C) Click again in the open doorway. Now you're standing outside the door of the synagogue.

8. GET YOUR BEARINGS.

(A) Look at the Thumbnail Map in the corner. The yellow dot indicates your location. The whitish triangle shows your field of vision.

On the Map, notice the blue path that starts at the bottom, at the Pool of Siloam, and proceeds north toward the Temple Mount. But you are at a crossroads. Ahead of you is a side street that heads west into a residential section of Jerusalem.

(B) On the main screen, drag right to look up the main road. (Notice how the whitish triangle has shifted on the Thumbnail Map.)

Just around that bend, you would see the temple, rising high. That's a great tour to take, but not right now—let's keep it simple.

(C) Drag right again to view the entrance of the synagogue, where you just were. Look, there's another green diamond. Click on it and see what happens. Afterwards click on the **BACK** button to return to the tour.

(D) Drag right once again to look down the street. Jerusalem is definitely a city set on a hill. All streets seem to go up or down. Notice the water of the Pool of Siloam. Notice

PART 1: USING *ILUMINA* ©
EXPERIENCING THE MEDIA CENTER

⊕ *When you click the Point in Time button, the scene will come to life and the freeze, allowing you to continue to look around.*

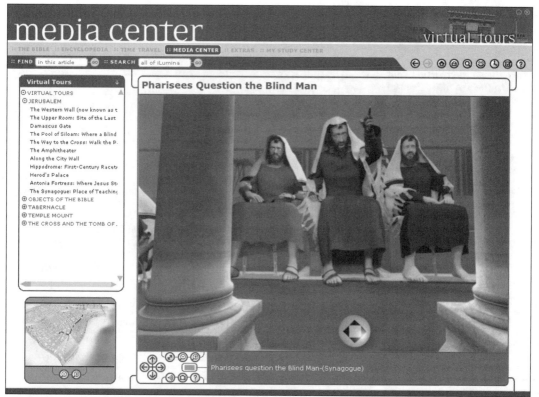

the walls of the city. Check your location again on the Thumbnail Map.

(E) Drag to the right one more time to get back where you started, looking up the side road that leads west.

9. MOVE UP THE SIDE STREET TWO POSITIONS.

(A) Make sure you're headed west up the side street, and not north toward the temple. Check the whitish triangle on the Thumbnail Map to confirm this.

(B) Click near the center of the screen. You can mouse around here a little, but there's nowhere to go but up.

(C) Click again near the center of the screen.

(D) Check your position on the Thumbnail Map.

Notice that the program has automatically turned you southward, because that's the only way to go. If you drag right 360 degrees, you'll see that the road continues westward and upward, but you can't take that. (That's where the rich folks live.) Another road heads north, but that's not part of our tour either. What we want to do is take this little side spur south.

10. MOVE SOUTH ALONG THIS SMALL STREET.

(A) Check the Thumbnail Map to make sure the whitish triangle has you looking south.

(B) Click near the center of the screen.

You are standing in front of a first-century dwelling. (Notice from the Thumbnail that the program has automatically turned you westward to face the house.) You can mouse around to see the road you walked on and where it continues, but our next move is inside this house.

11. ENTER THE HOUSE AND LOOK AROUND.

(A) Click on the open doorway.

The program has made you turn left, once inside the door.

(B) Drag to the left to see the doorway you just entered.

(C) Continue dragging left to view the atrium of this typical home. There's a staircase leading up to a guest room, an open area probably used as a stable, some first-floor rooms, and then another staircase, leading up to the main (upper) room.

SECRET

Take the Guided Virtual Tour to Galilee and around the sea to Kursi, the place where Jesus sent the demons into pigs. You can look around the churchyard there and find a bench. Click on it and you'll see why our tour guides can't afford to relax, even for a moment.

SECRET

Take the Guided Virtual Tour to the Sea of Galilee. An early stop there is Tabgha, where Jesus called his disciples. See the church and the sea and notice in the distance a small pier extending into the lake. Click on it to see some moments when our intelligent tour guides were all wet.

12. CLIMB THE STAIRS.

(A) Check the Thumbnail Map to make sure you're looking south. You want the staircase that's to your left as you enter the atrium.

(B) Click on the stairs. That puts you on the stairs.

(C) Click again on the stairs.

You have turned right, and you're facing the doorway to the main room of this house. But before you enter . . .

13. LOOK AROUND.

(A) Drag right and a little down, to see the steps you just climbed and the atrium.

(B) Continue dragging right until you see the open door to the atrium.

(C) Then drag up a little. That's the temple you see in the distance. And the city wall extending down the hill.

(D) Continue dragging right to complete your 360—you should once again be facing the door to the main room.

⊕ *What biblical event might have happened in this room?*

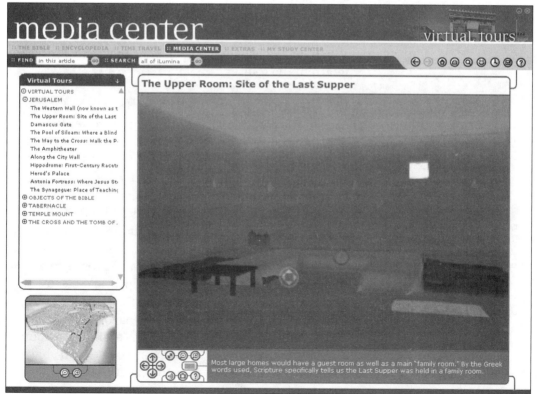

14. ENTER THE ROOM AND LOOK AROUND.

(A) Click on the open doorway.

Now you're in the room, and the program has made a right turn for you. You are facing a dining area with the low tables at which people reclined in those days.

(B) Drag left to see the steps leading to the roof. We'll take those later.

(C) Drag right again to look at the dining area.

(D) Click on the center of the screen to approach the table.

You are now in the center of this U-shaped table, and it looks like you've reclined there. You might mouse around to get your bearings, but hey, there's a green diamond. What biblical event might have happened in this room?

15. ENTER THE POINT IN TIME

(A) Click on the green diamond.

(B) Mouse around this scene to learn about the different elements of the Last Supper and some of the people who were there.

(C) Remember, you can drag the mouse around this scene, just as in any other spot on the Virtual Tour.

(D) When you've had enough, click the diamond again to return to the tour.

16. HIT THE ROOF

(A) Back in the empty upper room, drag left to see the doorway and the staircase.

(B) Click on the staircase. *You approach the stairs.*

(C) Click again on the stairs. *You climb the stairs.*

(D) Click on some point on the roof. *You walk out on the roof.*

(E) Now click-and-drag to your heart's content. This is as great a view of first-century Jerusalem as you'll ever see.

Our guided tour ends here. Of course, you're free to move around on your own. Perhaps you'd like to retrace your steps, moving down the stairs to the room, to the atrium, to the street, to the synagogue, and then up the hill to the temple. Or take one of the other tours available on the Index. But we hope you've been able to practice your touring skills through this little exercise.

Go to the Virtual Tour of Capernaum. You want to be in the first-century town, and go to the shore of the Sea of Galilee. You should see two boats on the water. One has a sphere on it, indicating you can click there to get gobs of good guidance about the goings-on of Galilee. If you click on the *other* boat, you'll get the bloopers. Apparently our guides don't always have both oars in the water.

From the roof of the upper-room house, you see the temple complex in the northeast. On the left corner of that structure is the "pinnacle" of the temple. Click on that, and *iLumina* will whisk you right there.

A Sunday School Teacher's New Curriculum

When she was teaching seven year olds, Lynette was in heaven. She had a sweetly effective way of communicating with her second-grade Sunday school class. The kids loved her, and she loved them. "Maybe it's because I still think on their level," she joked.

That's why it was such a disaster when they moved her to fifth grade. There was a new Sunday school superintendent whose wife wanted to teach second grade, and the fifth-grade teacher suddenly took a leave of absence due to a nervous breakdown. (The Sunday school class didn't *cause* the break-down, but it certainly didn't help.) It was decided that Lynette would be moved up three grades. She didn't have a lot of say in the matter. Oh, maybe she could have said no, but then she'd be letting down these poor teacherless children and, in a way, the entire church; she didn't need that kind of guilt heaped upon her.

So Lynette went into week one with a bad attitude, and maybe the kids caught it. Week after week, it was a struggle to win their attention. There were nine or ten of them, and Lynette had taught several of them just three years earlier. They'd been so sweet back then, but now they were, well, not *bad* exactly, just easily distracted. One day, seeing Sara Healy chatting and giggling with the girl next to her, Lynette paused and said, "Please don't talk while I'm teaching!" And little Sara stopped in mid-sentence to say, "I'm not talking"—*and then went back to her conversation*!

How could Lynette ever get through to them? They were starting a new quarter on Heroes of the Old Testament, and Lynette found herself browsing desperately through a Christian bookstore looking for anything that would capture her class. When she saw Goliath staring at her from an *iLumina* display, she knew she'd come to the right place. *This is just the guy I need on my side,* she thought.

At first she hoped that *iLumina* contained a hologram of the nine-foot giant, which she could project in class to terrify the kids into behaving. She found something much better. Lynette had often wondered how she could ever hope to compete with all the visual media her students were used to. For thirty hours a day, it seemed, they were watching action on screens—TV, movies, computer games, the Internet. No wonder she couldn't capture their attention! But maybe this computer program would enable her to fight fire with fire.

She arranged for one of the church's computers to be moved into her Sunday school class, and she loaded *iLumina* on it. Soon her students were seeing Moses' birth and the burning bush. Her students crowded in, drawn to the animation. She asked questions about how Moses must have felt, and then she played the scene again. They had a great discussion. The kids understood the story better now that they had seen it.

The next week, their topic was Joshua. They had no animation to look at, but Lynette planned a lesson built around maps, photos, and a brief Virtual Tour of the Tabernacle. It wasn't as easy, but the kids stayed pretty attentive.

Their next hero was David, so Lynette fired up the account of David and Goliath. The class loved this, even more than the Moses animations, perhaps because they could see that David wasn't much older than they were. Then they jumped into the scene via the Point in Time button, and started mousing around to learn about different parts of the story.

When the class time ended, the kids didn't want to leave, but Lynette paused the animation and shooed them off to the worship service. Turning back to the screen, she saw the scowling face of Goliath paused there. "Thanks, big guy," she smirked as she exited the program.

EXPERIENCING POINTS IN TIME

A Point in Time is sort of a cross between an animation and a Virtual Tour, as you saw if you took our guided tour above. You have the opportunity to enter a frame of an animation and move around in it, as you would in a Virtual Tour.

SELECTING A POINT IN TIME

If you've selected **POINTS IN TIME** in the Media Center Welcome screen, you will see a default frame on your screen, with the title and Bible reference at the top. You could start working with that scene if you like, or go to the Index window at the left, which now lists all the Points in Time available. The Index might just list locations, such as Jerusalem or Elah, but when you click on the name of that location, specific Points in Time will unfurl below it. (Elah, for instance, offers two scenes of David's encounter with Goliath.)

Once you've clicked on the name of a specific Point in Time, that scene will load up in the center of your screen, and you'll hear a line from that scene. (Be sure your computer's speakers are turned on.) You can Dragging and zooming in and out to move around the scene.

ENTERING POINTS IN TIME FROM ANIMATIONS

If you're watching an animation, and the diamond on the control panel begins to blink, that's your chance to enter that scene in a Point in Time. Just click that flashing diamond. When you're ready, the **BACK** button will bring you back to the animation.

⊕ *The different Points in Time available are listed in the Index window on the left side of the Points in Time screen.*

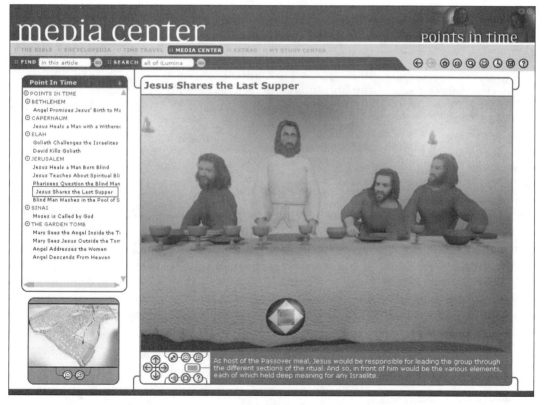

Generally, if a Point in Time is located in Jerusalem (including the Garden Tomb), you can move from that scene into the rest of the city on a Virtual Tour. The other Points in Time are in fixed locations that don't link to Virtual Tours.

ENTERING POINTS IN TIME FROM VIRTUAL TOURS

Or you might see a green diamond icon on a Virtual Tour. That means that a biblical story happened in this very spot, and you can enter a Point in Time at that location. Click on the green diamond to enter the Point in Time, and click the diamond again to get back.

MOVING THROUGH A POINT IN TIME

The basic skill needed is the click-and-drag. That is, click the mouse, and hold the clicker down while you move the mouse left or right, forward or back. The screen perspective will change, as if you were turning your head. You can also use the buttons on the Control bar (or your SHIFT and CTRL keys) to zoom in or out, giving the impression of walking forward or backward. However, extreme zoom-ins will look odd.

Navigating a Point in Time is the same as navigating a Virtual Tour. So read the preceding section on Virtual Tours to become an expert in the necessary skills.

Some Points in Time have a single setting. You can look around and zoom in and out, but you can't move to different positions. You can only click the diamond to return to the Virtual Tour. Other Points in Time, however, allow you to step out of the immediate location. You can leave the Last Supper to go up to the roof. You can brush past Mary in Jesus' tomb to walk out into the garden. You can leave Jesus with the blind man and enter the temple. If you do any of those things, you automatically leave the Point in Time and enter a Virtual Tour at that point. When you turn back to your previous location, the people will be gone.

In either of the David-and-Goliath Points in Time, click on the figure of Goliath. You'll see an "object movie" of the giant and his armor.

VIEWING BIBLE PHOTOS

If you click on **BIBLE PHOTOS** in the Media Center Welcome screen, a photo will appear in the center of your screen and an alphabetical index in the left-side panel. There are hundreds of photos of biblical sites available to you.

SELECTING A PHOTO

Scroll through the Index window on the left until you find the title of the photo you want. You could also use the **FIND** space to search for a particular word or name in a photo title. This could be especially helpful if you're looking for various photos from Ephesus, for instance. Type in "Ephesus" and you'll find an amphitheater, a fountain, a library building, and other pictures from that site.

Click on the title of any photo you want to view.

USING THE PHOTO VIEWER AND PHOTO CONTROL BAR

The center of the screen gives you a nice, wide space to see the photos you've chosen. The title is always at the top left, and a caption for the photo is centered at its bottom.

Directly beneath the photo, you'll see the Photo Control bar. The **SNAPSHOT** button is very useful with photos. Click there to copy the image to your computer clipboard to use with other graphics programs or in My Study Center (see page 72). The rectangle icon is the **THEATER** button. Click this to enlarge the photo into Theater Mode, which will fill up your screen. The **HELP** button stands there like a loyal servant, always ready to be of assistance.

PLEASE NOTE: If you take a snapshot of a photo and use it for anything beyond your own personal viewing pleasure, you *must* look at the permission information for *iLumina*. (To view this, click the **HELP** button and click on **CREDITS**, then

In the "Angel Descends from Heaven" Point in Time, you see four Roman soldiers terrified by this celestial being. Click on the second one from the right to get an up-close look at the garb of Roman soldiers.

⊕ iLumina's *extensive library of biblical photos is easily accessible in the Media Center.*

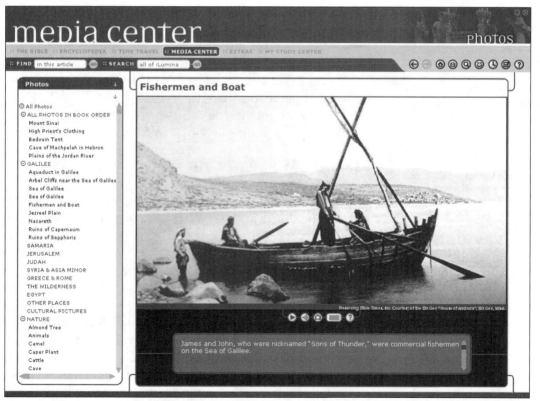

NOTE

Look for the photo credit line immediately under the right side of the photo. If you take a snapshot of a photo and reuse it in any way, make sure that credit line is copied, too. It's the legal thing to do. But any photographs with the following credit line: "Preserving Bible Times, Inc. 'Reproduction of the City of Jerusalem at the time of the Second Temple located on the grounds of the Holyland Hotel, Jerusalem' " *must not be reproduced in any way whatsoever.*

SECRET

Go on your own through the Virtual Tour of Jerusalem. Find your way to the amphitheater. (You could just click The Amphitheater on the index but how adventurous would that be?) The amphitheater is west of the Temple Mount and a bit south of the city wall. In any case, you want to be *outside* the theater, exploring the neighboring houses. Enter the house next door, and you'll be able to go behind the scenes of this whole *iLumina* operation.

PERMISSION INFO. Or just search the Help Index for "credits.") *In general*, anything in *iLumina* can be copied and shared with church groups of 50 or less, but some credit lines are required and **THERE ARE SOME PHOTOS THAT CANNOT BE REPRODUCED AT ALL.** Check the Permission Info for the full explanation.

STUDYING THE BIBLE ATLAS

When you click on **BIBLE ATLAS** in the Media Center Welcome screen, a map appears in the center of your screen with an index in the left-side panel. You've got a whole Bible atlas available to you.

SELECTING A MAP

Appearing in that left-side panel, the basic map index is in Bible order. Maps that pertain to Genesis are at the beginning and a map showing the seven churches of Revelation is at the end. If you want maps covering a certain portion of Scripture, scroll down to that book of the Bible and look for a map that will help you.

But there are also other categories in the index. Click on the index title bar to see what your options are. You could see lists of the maps pertaining to Jerusalem or Jesus, Apostles or Kings.

You could also use the **FIND** space to search for a particular word or name in a map title.

When you find the title of a map you want to look at, click on that title. The map will appear in the main viewing area.

USING THE MAP VIEWER, THE MAPS CONTROL BAR, AND THE MAP THUMBNAIL

You're looking at the map you've selected in the center of the screen. The title is at the top left, and there might be a Bible reference (click to link to it) at top right. A caption for the map appears at the bottom.

To the left of the caption area is the Maps Control bar. Top left, you'll find the plus and minus signs, the **ZOOM CONTROLS**, which can zoom in or out on the map image. Below those controls, you'll find the four **DIRECTIONAL ARROWS**. As you might guess, these help you position the map in the viewing area. Many of the maps are too large to fit the space, and that's especially true if you've zoomed in at all. At the right are our familiar media controls: the **SNAPSHOT** button, which lets you copy the map image to your computer clipboard for future use; the **THEATER** button, which lets you view the map in a wide-screen format; and the ever-agreeable **HELP** button.

At the bottom left of your screen is the **MAP THUMB-NAIL**. This gives you a tiny image of the entire map, indicating the portion of it that you are viewing in your main screen. This is especially helpful if you have zoomed in on an area and want to keep a sense of the larger context. You can move the square in the Map Thumbnail over the map, and you will see the portion of the map within the square centered in the viewing area.

VIEWING MEDIA IN THEATER MODE

Each of the five formats in the Media Center can be viewed in Theater Mode—Animations, Virtual Reality, Points in Time, Photos, and Maps. While you lose immediate access to the index and any thumbnails, you get a much broader view.

SECRET

In the Virtual Tours, the house next to the Jerusalem amphi- theater is your portal to the office where *iLumina* was created (see page 58). Once there, you can start by looking around the planning room. This is where many of the ideas were hatched, or at least argued about. Find a verse posted on the wall and click on that. See where it takes you. You can always click the back button to get back to this room.

⊕ *The maps in the Bible Atlas, like most of* iLumina*'s media, can be viewed in Theater Mode.*

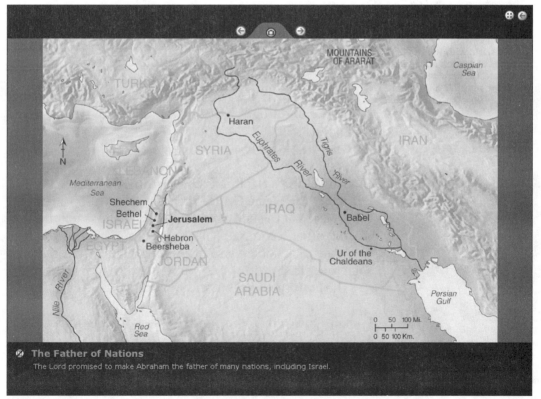

The Father of Nations
The Lord promised to make Abraham the father of many nations, including Israel.

USING THE THEATER MODE MEDIA BAR

In Theater Mode, title and caption appear at the bottom of the viewing area, with the Media bar at the top. To the left and right of the familiar Media bar elements are an arrow pointing left and another pointing right. The left-pointing arrow will take you directly to the previous image in your current index. That is, whatever type of media you're viewing, it will go back to that index and load up the previous map, photo, animation, or whatever. The right-pointing arrow loads up the *next* one in that index.

The other controls on the Media bar will vary slightly, depending on which medium is loaded. All of them will include the **SNAPSHOT** button, allowing you to save the image to your computer clipboard for future use.

When you are watching an Animation in Theater Mode, you have the three standard buttons plus a **PLAY/PAUSE** button, a **STOP** button, a **PROGRESS SLIDER**, a **VOLUME** button, and a **POINTS IN TIME** button, which will flash whenever you get to a point in an animation where a Point in Time is available.

When you are exploring a Virtual Tour or a Point in Time, you have **ZOOM** controls and a **VOLUME** button. (If you have any questions about these controls, go back to the section on that particular medium.)

In the upper right corner of your screen are two buttons that can get you back to civilization. The purplish button takes you to the part of the Media Center that contains the type of media you're viewing—whether it's photos or animations. The **BACK** button will take you back to wherever you came from.

TIP

The left and right arrows might seem confusing, but try using them to connect animations that are part of the same story. Load up "Jesus Heals the Blind Man" and, when it's finished, click the right arrow, and do that once again. You get three stories back to back, giving you all of John 9. You could do the same with the double-stories of David and Goliath and Jesus' Resurrection, or with the multiple animations regarding the Tabernacle.

LINKING TO THE REST OF *ILUMINA*

On any of the Media Center screens, you may find a few buttons stacked at the bottom right. These are links to other media and other sections of *iLumina*. Click on one and you'll go to a particular Bible verse or article or animation that has something to do with what you're currently viewing.

The basic sectional buttons look like this:

Look for the color-coding on these sectional buttons:

BLUE: Bible
RED: Encyclopedia
GOLD: Time Travel

CHAPTER SEVEN

⊖ TAPPING INTO *ILUMINA'S* EXTRAS

TO GET TO THE EXTRAS, click **EXTRAS** on the *iLumina* home page.

OR, you can also reach the Extras from any other screen by clicking on **EXTRAS** in the menu bar.

You will see a screen that tells you all sorts of glowing things about *iLumina*. Read that and think about how fortunate you are to be using *iLumina* at this very moment! When the glow fades, glance over to the Index window at the left. There you see a list detailing the available extras.

PURCHASING *ILUMINA* PRODUCTS

The first version of *iLumina (1.0)* hit the stores in the fall of 2002, and shortly after that a minor upgrade (1.1) was available at the *iLumina* Web site. As of the fall of 2003, two newer versions became available.

iLumina (2.0) is a significant step up from version 1.1, with a sharper visual design and sleeker programming. And it's amazingly affordable.

iLumina Gold is the deluxe edition with many more resources available, including a parallel Bible translation, and the My Study Center feature.

If you already have *iLumina 1.0* or *2.0*, the *iLumina Gold Upgrade* can get you humming along at the deluxe level.

To order any of these products, click on the product name under "The World of *iLumina*" in the Extras Index window.

⊕ *The Extras screen provides links to* iLumina *Customer Service.*

UPGRADING TO *ILUMINA* GOLD

If you have already purchased *iLumina* (1.0, 1.1, or 2.0), you can go to www.iLumina.com to learn more about the exciting features of *iLumina Gold*, including My Study Center advanced searches and stunning Guided Virtual Tours. You can buy the *iLumina Gold Upgrade* wherever Bible software is sold. If you are having trouble locating an *iLumina Gold Upgrade* at your local bookstore or software retailer, go to the customer service section of www.iLumina.com and write us a note. We'll be here to assist you.

GETTING FUTURE UPDATES ON THE INTERNET

The *iLumina* adventure is just beginning. At this writing, a special upgrade for church leaders is in the works, and they're talking about another *iLumina* upgrade for family use. Various Christian organizations are talking about creating special editions of *iLumina* for their specific needs. And who knows what additional bells and whistles might be downloadable in the near future.

To connect to the *iLumina* Web site and learn all the latest possibilities, click on www.iLumina.com.

TAKING A BEHIND-THE-SCENES LOOK AT *ILUMINA*

How was *iLumina* created? Who did all those cool animations? What do the *iLumina*-makers eat for breakfast? Do they even *have* breakfast? For the answers to some of these questions, click on **BEHIND THE SCENES** under "The World of *iLumina*" in the Extras Index window.

FINDING ANSWERS TO FREQUENTLY ASKED QUESTIONS

Why does this always do this? Why won't it do this? How can I get it to do this? Already you've been coming up with questions about how *iLumina* operates. You can quickly get answers to the most common queries by clicking on **FAQS ABOUT *ILUMINA*** under "Contact Us" in the Extras Index window.

CONTACTING *ILUMINA* TECH SUPPORT

If your question is not addressed in the FAQs section, you can contact *iLumina* Tech Support via the Internet. To find out how, click on **CONTACT TECH SUPPORT** under "Contact Us" in the Extras Index window.

CONTACTING *ILUMINA* CUSTOMER SERVICE

If you have some service issue—say the *iLumina* package is missing a disk, or the box has graffiti all over it (not that any of those things would *really happen*, mind you)—you can contact Customer Service. Click on **CONTACT CUSTOMER SERVICE** under "Contact Us" in the Extras Index window.

WHEN YOU NEED HELP

1. Click on the HELP command on the *iLumina* Toolbar, or in any of the Media bars you run across.

2. If "Help" isn't helpful enough, try FAQs ABOUT *ILUMINA* under Contact Us in the Extras Index window. If your question is "frequently asked" enough, you will find your answer there.

3. If you still haven't found the answer, click on TECH SUPPORT under Contact Us in the Extras Index window. Then you can send an S.O.S. to an *iLumina* techie.

4. If you have a problem with the product itself—the packaging, the contents, the service, or anything like that— try CONTACT CUSTOMER SERVICE under Contact Us in the Extras Index window. Those customer service reps will do lots of nice things for you, but they can't make *iLumina* run better on your computer. Only the tech support team can do that.

CHAPTER EIGHT

⊙ CREATING DOCUMENTS IN MY STUDY CENTER

TO GET TO My Study Center, click **MY STUDY CENTER** on the *iLumina* home page.

OR, you can also reach My Study Center from any other screen by clicking on **MY STUDY CENTER** in the menu bar.

You will see the Welcome screen for My Study Center, which describes how to use My Study Center before giving you the **START NOW** link.

UNDERSTANDING HOW MY STUDY CENTER WORKS

Perhaps you are using *iLumina* to prepare Sunday school lessons and sermons, or to write papers and create handouts. You want to process the great material of *iLumina* for your own purposes. Now you can. My Study Center gives you the opportunity to pull together different elements of *iLumina* into a single document that you can print and save.

Imagine a desktop with three sections. Let's say you're an executive interviewing people for a job in your company. On the left is a stack of applications and resumes—you have lots to choose from. You take a folder from that stack, open it up, and spread it out in front of you. You look at all the information about that candidate, and you decide whether you can use this person in your company. If you decide you can, you turn to the right side of your desk and write a recommendation to send to the personnel manager. Three sections: Search, Display, My Study.

My Study Center is that desktop. It has three panels across, *but you can only see two of them at a time.* Yet those three sections function much like the executive's workspace: a stack of search info on the left; an evaluation area in the center; and,

NOTE

In order to keep *iLumina* affordable, the My Study Center feature was not included. This feature is only in *iLumina Gold*. But *iLumina* users might still find it useful to look through this chapter. Or maybe it will inspire you to save up for a Gold Upgrade.

looking to the right, you find an area where you can create a document with the info you've selected. Search. Display. My Study.

If you are looking at the Search/Display tandem, just click on the huge arrow at the right to slide right. Then you'll be looking at the Display/My Study screen but you can slide left by clicking on the huge arrow at the left. You'll probably go back and forth many times as you process material for your document.

GATHERING MATERIAL

Do you need Bible verses for that lesson you're preparing? No problem. *iLumina* has plenty. You want to use a paragraph from the Encyclopedia? You got it. But what if you're preparing a handout for your second-grade Sunday school class and you'd love to print out a frame of that David and Goliath animation? You can do that too. Virtually all of *iLumina*'s contents can be clipped and pasted into whatever document you choose.

USING THE ADVANCED SEARCH

Let's say you're preparing a talk on the Atonement. You want to search Scripture for all the verses on that subject. In the Bible section, you can do a simple word search for "atonement" and come up with a few verses. But here in My Study Center you can do more serious searching.

You can open the Advanced Search dialog box by clicking **ADVANCED SEARCH** in the Study bar under the menu bar at the top. The Advanced Search is designed to find exactly what you want and not what you don't want. If you learn to use the various spaces in this dialog box, you can narrow down your search and save a lot of time. Here's what options are available to you:

With All These Words
Type any words, in any order, into this box. My Study Center will search *iLumina* for any Bible verse or Encyclopedia article that contains *all* the words you typed.

With This Exact Phrase
Type into this box a phrase you want to search for. Be sure to type the phrase exactly, because My Study Center will search *iLumina* for the exact text you entered.

With Any of These Words
Type any words, in any order, into this box. My Study Center will search *iLumina* for any search unit that contains any one or more of the words you typed.

Without These Words

Type any words you want to *exclude* from your search into this box. My Study Center will search *iLumina* for any search unit that contains the words or phrases you entered into the other boxes *and does not contain* any of the words you typed into this box.

Match Case

Check this box if you want to search for the words or phrases you entered and match the uppercase or lowercase letters. Leave this box unchecked if you don't want your search to be case-sensitive. For example, if you type "god" into the search

℗ *My Study Center makes it easy to gather topically related material and view it in context.*

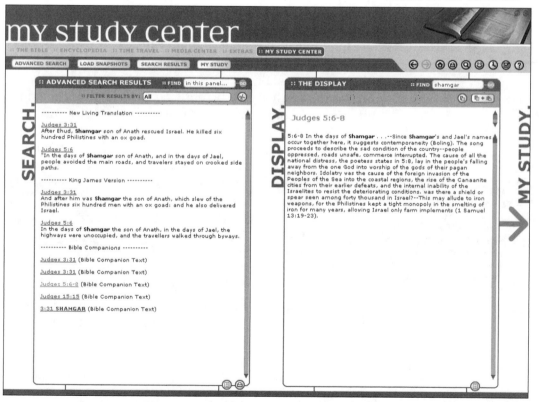

TIP

Generally case doesn't matter in word searches, so you could leave the "Match Case" box unchecked. But if you're studying Bible occupations and you search for "job," you'll get just about every verse in Job. The case could also distinguish between Noah's ark and the Ark of the Covenant.

box and *don't* check the "Match Case" box, the search will yield all appearances of "God" and "god." But if you're looking for cases of people worshiping a false god, it might be a good idea to check the "Match Case" box to get only those entries (and avoid wading through the seven million mentions of "God" in the Bible).

Go

Click this button when you're ready to begin your search. You might have to wait several seconds. Some of the more complicated searches may take more time.

Cancel

Click this button to close the dialog box without executing your search.

Help

Click this to go to *iLumina's* on-board help system.

Simple

Click this button to return the dialog box to the simple Search dialog, without all these extra options.

Search Locations

If you don't specify anything, the entire content of *iLumina* will be searched: Bible, notes, Encyclopedia, Time Travel, media captions and titles. If you search everything in *iLumina*, be prepared to wait awhile because *iLumina* contains thousands of pages of commentaries, Bible studies, charts, and Bible texts. Maybe that's exactly what you want; maybe not. Perhaps you'd prefer to start with just the Bible text, then look through Encyclopedia articles, and so on. Perhaps you've prepared your lesson, but you're looking for some media elements to include. In any case, you can narrow the search by clicking the **CHECK/UNCHECK ALL** button and then selectively checking the areas you want to search.

WE'VE GOT SCROLL
You probably figured this out, but the Search area is *scrollable*. Some of your searches might return hundreds of items. Use the scroll bar at the right of the Search panel to look at them all.

SEARCHING BIBLE TEXT

If you didn't read the last few paragraphs above on "Using the Advanced Search," shame on you! Seriously, though, you may want to dog-ear the page so you can come back later and take full advantage of the power the advanced search features offer. Now we're going to use some of these features to search the Bible.

To search just the Bible text, go to the Search Locations spot in the Advanced Search dialog box and make sure that only the Bible listing is checked. Then go up to the Selection bar, just under the title bar of the Search panel. Click on **FILTER RESULTS BY** to select the Bible version you want (New Living Translation or King James Version).

Then type in a word or phrase you want to search for and click **GO**. If you don't already have a phrase in mind, try "grace and peace be yours". In a few seconds you should have a list of Bible verses in the Search area with your target word or phrase in bold type. (To begin working with these verses, see "Displaying the Context of Your Search" below.)

SEARCHING OTHER *ILUMINA* SECTIONS

Searching just Encyclopedia articles or any other part of *iLumina* is easy. Just use the same basic procedure as you did for the Bible search. Go to the Search Locations spot in the Advanced Search dialog box and check the section or sections you'd like to search. If some timeline info would look great in your paper for history class, search the Time Travel section. If you want to share a map with your Bible study group, activate the Media Center search. Type in the word or phrase you

☺ *If you want to search just one section of* iLumina, *like the Encyclopedia for instance, make sure to check only that box in the Advanced Search dialog box.*

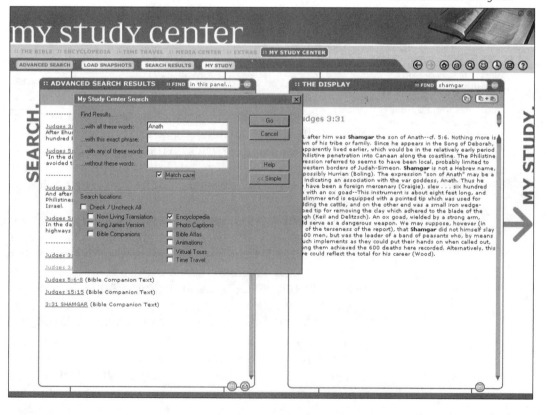

want to search for and click **GO**. As your searches get more complex you may need to reference the directions and information under "Using the Advanced Search" above.

After you click **GO**, the Search area on the left half of your screen will fill up with titles of any media elements or other items it has found. You might even see a line of a caption or blurb with your target words or phrases in bold. (To see the whole item, see "Displaying the Context of Your Search" below.)

PROCESSING SEARCH RESULTS

The Search is just the beginning. Now you'll need to sift through the search results to get the verses, articles, or media elements you can use.

FILTERING THE SEARCH RESULTS

You can do a second search *within* your search results by using the **FIND** space in the title bar of the Search panel. Say you searched for *love* (haven't we all?) and you came up with a list of hundreds of entries, each containing the word "love" in bold type. You could then go to the **FIND** space and type in "world", and suddenly every mention of the word "world" will also be in bold.

Note: The **FIND** function will not crunch your list. It won't delete anything. It will just highlight the target word within your search results.

If you searched "all of *iLumina*," or several sections, you can now filter your search, taking one section at a time. After your search results appear, click on the **FILTER BAR**, just below the title bar for this Search panel. A drop-down menu will list the different sections of *iLumina* that were searched. Click on any of those to see results from just that section.

For instance, you might be preparing a Sunday school lesson on the topic of prayer. You search all of *iLumina*, and get a substantial list of results. Now you want to start by just looking at some key Bible verses on the subject. So you'll click on **FILTER RESULTS BY** and choose **BIBLE** in order to display only the results found in the Bible section of *iLumina*. Note that you can also filter by Bible *version* (NLT or KJV). Then, after you've selected some key verses, you might want to examine the results from the Encyclopedia. Click on **FILTER RESULTS BY** and choose **ENCYCLOPEDIA** to focus on that listing.

TIP

The FIND function in the Search area is great for afterthoughts. *I've got this list of every biblical mention of grace. Hmmm. How many of these verses also mention faith?* But if you're doing a serious study of grace and faith, it's better to type them both in the Advanced Search box to begin with.

DELETING ENTRIES

Chances are, your search will yield a list that's bigger than you need. You can prune your list by using the **DELETE** command in the Filter bar underneath the title bar of the Search panel. Just highlight the verse you want to get rid of (by dragging the cursor down through the text), and click **DELETE**. It's gone.

PRINTING YOUR SEARCH RESULTS

In most cases, you'll be processing the search results here in My Study Center. But who knows? You might want to print out the list and go to your local café, where you'll pick and choose the Bible verses you want to use while enjoying a steamy cup of joe. You can do that. You pick the café, *iLumina* prints out the search results, and you're off.

Go to the lower right edge of the Search panel and click the **PRINT** button there. Assuming your computer is hooked up to a working printer, a printer dialog box should show up and ask you whether you want to print a snapshot of the screen or just the search results. In this case, you want just the

⊕ *The printer dialog box.*

search results. A second dialog box will then pop up, so you can tell your printer what to do. Your printer will churn out the contents of the search panel only—just the search results, no Display or My Study contents.

Be careful though. A search might produce thousands of entries. That might take hundreds of pages to print. If you want to save a few trees, and your paper supply, be sure your search results are a manageable size before you print.

SAVING YOUR SEARCH RESULTS

You can also save your search results by clicking **SEARCH RESULTS** on the Study bar, and clicking **SAVE AS**. That will save the contents of the search panel only (including all its scrollable contents, but nothing from the Display or My Study panels). You will be asked to name the file you save.

LOADING PREVIOUSLY SAVED SEARCH RESULTS

When you come back to My Study Center, you can load previously saved search results by clicking **SEARCH RESULTS** on the Study bar, and clicking **LOAD**. You will be asked for the name of the file you want.

DELETING THE WHOLE LIST OF SEARCH RESULTS

If you're finished with your list and you want to start over, you can delete the entire list by clicking **SEARCH RESULTS** on the Study bar, and clicking **DELETE**. Make sure you're really finished with it, because it will be gone.

DISPLAYING THE CONTEXT OF YOUR SEARCH

The Search panel gives you the minimal content of your Search results—every mention of your target word or phrase in your selected medium. But in order to do any meaningful work with this information, you need the bigger picture. You need *context*. That's why My Study Center has that Display panel on the right half of your screen.

Simply click on the Bible reference above any Bible verse on your list, and the entire Bible chapter will pop up in the Display area, with your selected verse at the top. Scroll up or down to read the whole context. If you have a list of Encyclopedia articles, click on any title and the whole article will appear in the Display area. Scroll up or down as necessary. If your list includes other media elements of *iLumina*, just click on a title and that element—picture, map, animation frame—will appear in the Display panel. The same goes for Snapshots.

If you're displaying text, the Display area functions like other text areas in *iLumina*: you can highlight and copy text, right-click on any word to look it up, and even search within that text for other words or phrases (using the **FIND** space at the top).

If you're displaying a media element, the Display panel becomes a Media window, with a control bar. (See page 39 for details on this Media bar.)

Only one Bible chapter, Encyclopedia article, or media element can appear in the Display area at any given time. If you click on another title in the Search area, the displayed piece will be replaced by the new one.

So examine the text or image being displayed, and decide whether you might use it. If so, you'll want to transfer it to your workspace. You can do this automatically, by clicking **COPY AND PASTE** in the Study bar. That will send any highlighted text or any media image to the My Study panel even if you're not viewing that panel at the moment. But if you want

⊕ *When your search results include multimedia, the Display panel will function like a Media window to show them to you.*

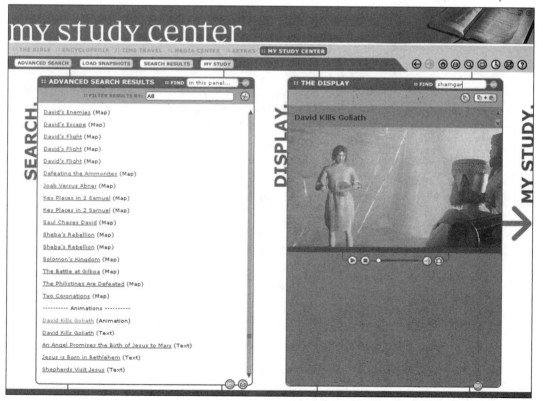

to see where you're pasting this material, click the big arrow pointing right on the right side of the Search/Display screen. That will slide you over to the right side of your "desktop." You still see the Display area, just as you left it, but now you have the My Study panel on the right. Here you can construct your document.

MOVING TEXT TO YOUR DOCUMENT

Once you have slid over to the Display/My Study screen, it's like cutting and pasting in any word processing program. If you have a Bible chapter or Encyclopedia article or other text in the Display area, you can select any portion of it (by clicking and dragging through it). Then click the **COPY AND PASTE** button in the Study bar. The selected text will appear in the My Study area. You can also click **COPY**, which places the text or image on your computer clipboard. Then you can position your cursor (by clicking on the page) exactly where you want the copied material, and then click the **PASTE** button at the top of the My Study panel.

TIP

Like a "paste" function in other word processors, the COPY AND PASTE button will put selected text *wherever the cursor is* in the My Study panel. That will usually be at the end of any previously pasted material. But if you want to paste new material in the middle of your document, place the cursor there.

LOADING SNAPSHOTS

If you've already been working with *iLumina*, perhaps you have taken a few Snapshots along the way. A photo you liked. A frame of a Bible animation. That spot in the Virtual Tour that took your breath away. To add some of those favorite snapshots to your document, use the big left-arrow to slide back over to the Search/Display screen. Now all you have to do is click on **LOAD SNAPHOTS** in the Selection bar just below the title bar of the Search panel.

That will give you a list of all the Snapshots you've taken. Click on a title, and you'll see that photo, map, or frame reproduced in the Display area.

MOVING MEDIA IMAGES TO YOUR DOCUMENT

If your Display area is showing some *still* media image, like a snapshot or photo for instance, and you want to use that in your document, just click the **COPY AND PASTE** button and the image will be copied to the My Study panel. (Or **COPY** for a later pasting.) Note that the My Study panel has two "pages," represented by tabs at the top—Text and Media. If you transfer a media image, the Media page automatically comes to the front. You can place multiple images on that page, but these can be viewed only one at a time.

Victor Leads Devotions

The assignment was simple enough——lead devotions for the stewardship committee——but Victor was beside himself. He was no preacher. One on one with a client, this CPA was a great communicator, but public speaking terrified him, even if that "public" consisted of five other committee members.

Still, they had agreed to start their meetings with devotions, and they were taking turns leading. Last month Jack Lascom had read the passage about the woman who poured perfume on Jesus' feet and offered a few comments. Victor thought that Jack seemed entirely too intrigued by the "sinful life" this woman had led, which took the talk in a somewhat awkward direction. Victor was determined to do better, but he wasn't sure how.

One thing about Victor: he was always prepared. For a week before the meeting, he obsessed about these devotions he would have to lead. Every night at the dinner table he asked his family for their opinions. Finally, Vic Jr. said, "Why don't you just use *iLumina*?"

Four months earlier, they had given Vic Jr. the program for his birthday. Quite the computer whiz, he had delighted in exploring everything that *iLumina* could do. He had even sent e-mails to *iLumina*'s creators, asking about glitches in the program, and suggesting improvements for the next upgrade. Now it was his pleasure to walk his dad through the My Study Center feature.

It was amazingly easy, actually. They searched for "Stewardship" and found an Encyclopedia article listed. When they clicked on that entry, the article appeared in the display area. This article contained a collection of Bible verses grouped into a few different thematic categories. "That's way more material than I can use," Victor exclaimed. "I guess I'll just have to pick a couple of the verses to share some thoughts on."

"Do you see any good ones?" asked Vic Jr. "Let's look them up and see the context."

Victor quickly looked over the Bible verses that were mentioned in the article. He noticed two verses listed from the same chapter, Proverbs 3. 'Let's look those up," he said. "I'll grab a Bible."

"No, Dad," Vic Jr. said, chuckling to himself. "This *is* a Bible." He clicked on a Bible reference and suddenly the text of Proverbs 3 was in front of them. As it turned out, that chapter was full of verses that Victor could use. Verse 9: "Honor the LORD with your wealth and with the best part of everything your land produces." Verse 21: "Don't lose sight of good planning and insight." Verse 26: "The LORD is your security." And verse 28: "If you can help your neighbor now, don't say, 'Come back tomorrow, and then I'll help you.' "

With Vic Jr.'s help, Victor copied the verses he wanted and pasted them into a document he started on the My Study screen of My Study Center. When he had all the verses he needed, he started organizing them and adding his own comments. Then he printed out the document.

And that's what he had in front of him as he led devotions for the Stewardship Committee. He was still nervous as he spoke, but he was well-prepared. "So it seems pretty clear," he said, concluding his talk, "that we must plan wisely, but we must also trust the Lord, rather than money, to protect us. And maybe we need to be a little more adventurous in helping our needy neighbors. We don't want to tell them, 'Come back next year, when it's in our budget.' We must honor the Lord *now* with all we have, because it really belongs to him. That's all."

There was a brief silence after Victor stopped speaking. People were looking at him and nodding their approval. The committee chairman smiled and said, "Very nice. Maybe we should ask you to fill in for the pastor next summer."

"Don't even joke about that," laughed Victor nervously.

The Display area might be showing an animation, or a frame of a Virtual Tour or Point in Time. In that case, use the Media Control bar to take a **SNAPSHOT** (the camera icon) of the exact frame you want. Then you can **COPY AND PASTE** the Snapshot to the My Study panel. You could possibly copy several different frames of an animation, Virtual Tour, or Point in Time.

When Media images are copied and pasted to the My Study panel, the captions don't go along for the ride. With the image you get only a title and copyright info. So if there is information within a caption that you want, you'll need to type that in to the Text page of the My Study panel.

WORKING WITH YOUR DOCUMENT

The My Study panel is a simple word-processor. You can type in it; copy, cut and paste; and use bold, italic, or underline type. You can also change the size of type to small, medium, or large. Use the scroll bar at the right to move up or down through the document, which can be as long as you want it to be.

If you want to "crop" a map, you will not be able to do so in the My Study panel. But you can use the Media Control bar to zoom in and position the image. Then take a Snapshot and copy that to the My Study panel.

⊕ *The My Study panel will allow you to paste information from your Display panel, add your own notes or comments, and then use bold, italics, or underlining in your document.*

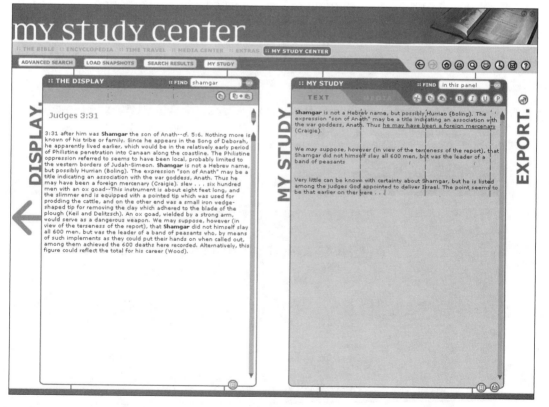

CREATING NEW TEXT

Just click on the page and start typing. You can start a new document or add your comments to text that you've moved over from the Display panel.

LOADING MATERIAL FROM ELSEWHERE IN *ILUMINA*

What if you don't need to search? Say you already know that Psalm 23 will be the centerpiece of your Bible study. You can load that into the My Study panel directly. Here's how.

In the menu bar up top, click **THE BIBLE**. Then use the **GO TO** command on the Search bar to call up the reference you want. Then, within the Bible text, highlight the verses you want to copy. Hold the CTRL key down and press C to copy it to the computer clipboard. Then, in the toolbar (top right), use the **BACK** command or the **HISTORY** button to get back to My Study Center. Click on the My Study panel to place your cursor on the right spot, and click the **PASTE** icon (or CTRL+V) to paste the verses you've copied.

This process also works for any Encyclopedia article or other text you find on your own.

In order to load in a media image without using a Search, take a Snapshot of that image wherever you find it. Then use the **LOAD SNAPSHOTS** command in the My Study Center Search panel, and click it across to the My Study panel.

EDITING TEXT

Use the buttons at the top of the My Study panel to edit text you've moved here or created. Highlight the text you want to change (by clicking and dragging through it) and then click on:

 CUT TEXT (CTRL+X) to Cut

COPY TEXT (CTRL+C) to Copy

 PASTE TEXT (CTRL+V) to Paste material you have just cut or copied

 COPY AND PASTE moves an item from the display panel to the My Study panel

BOLD TEXT (CTRL+B) to switch to Bold type

ITALICIZE TEXT (CTRL+I) to switch to Italicized type

UNDERLINE TEXT (CTRL+U) to switch to Underlined type

 PLAIN TEXT to switch back to a plain typeface

If you have written or copied a lot of text to this page, you might also need the **FIND** space at the top of the My Study panel. Type in a word or phrase that you are hunting for and click **GO**; it will find and highlight that text wherever it appears in this document.

This word processor is always in Insert mode (not Overtype). And any new text you move to the page will be placed wherever the cursor is.

WORKING WITH MEDIA ELEMENTS

You can also move pictures, maps, animation frames, and other media elements to this My Study panel. They will go to the Media page. You can toggle back and forth between the Media page and the Text page by clicking on the tabs at the top of the My Study panel.

TIP

The normal keyboard shortcuts that you find in many word-processing programs also apply here. Press the CTRL key with C to copy highlighted text, with X to cut it, and with V to paste text that's been cut or copied. CTRL+B makes highlighted text bold, CTRL+I makes it Italic, and CTRL+U underlines it.

⊕ *You can place any media element you desire in the My Study panel, although the Animations will appear only as still shots.*

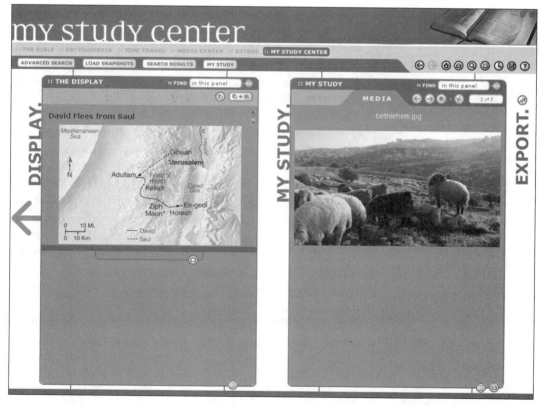

You can place multiple media images to this Media page, but they can only be viewed one at a time. If you have three images, a note will indicate that the current image is "1 of 3" and so on. You can change the image you're viewing by clicking the left and right arrows.

Although you can't edit media images here, you can export them to your computer. Then you can use other software to modify those images, if you like. In any modification you do, be sure to use the images in legal ways, by using them only in nonprofit and noncommercial teaching settings for groups under 50 and by not placing images on the Internet. Always keep the copyright information visible on a photo or image. The original creators of those images deserve that credit.

GETTING MORE MATERIAL FROM YOUR SEARCH

In most cases, you'll be working with more than one Bible text or Encyclopedia article. The whole point of My Study Center is to let you pull together information from different sources. There are a couple of methods you might use.

SLIDE STEPS

Let's say you've searched for "shepherd" and clicked on Psalm 23:1. You got all of Psalm 23 in the Display panel, and then you slid over to the My Study panel, highlighting and moving the first two verses of that psalm. Then you added some of your own brilliant prose about this image of God as shepherd. Now you want more.

So, slide back to the Search side of My Study Center by clicking on the big left-arrow on the left side of your screen. That puts you back in the Search/Display duplex, and your search results are just where you left them. Now you scroll down to find John 10:13, where Jesus says he is the good shepherd. Perfect. You click on that to see all of John 10 in the Display area. Good thing, because Jesus says some other pertinent things in the surrounding verses. You decide to use verses 9-13, so you hit the big right-arrow to slide over to the Edit panel. There's your Psalm 23 document, just as you left it. Making sure your cursor is placed where you want the new text, you highlight John 10:9-13 in the Display panel and click **COPY AND PASTE**. *Voila!* It appears in your document, and you add some ground-breaking commentary.

But now you need more info about sheep. Slide back to the Search/Display screen to grab some Encyclopedia copy about sheep and shepherds. Click the title and read the article. Then slide back to the right, select a few lines, and **COPY AND PASTE** them to the My Study panel.

You get the idea. You might slide back and forth five or ten times in constructing a document. It all stays on your "desktop" as you slide back and forth across the three panels.

DIG AND DUMP

But maybe all that sliding makes you dizzy. Then try the "dig and dump." In this method, you stay on the Search/Display side. Click on a reference or title in the Search panel, and look at the full chapter or article in the Display panel. Figure out what you'd like to use, highlight it, and click **COPY AND PASTE**. It will automatically be copied on the My Study panel. Trust us. You don't have to slide over and look at it; it's there. Then click on the next reference or title. Examine, choose, highlight, **COPY AND PASTE**.

Do that as many times as you want. When you've pasted everything you want, *then* slide over to your My Study panel. You've dumped a bunch of stuff there. Now you can start

® *When nothing is selected, clicking the Copy and Paste button will paste the entire contents of the Display panel into the My Study panel.*

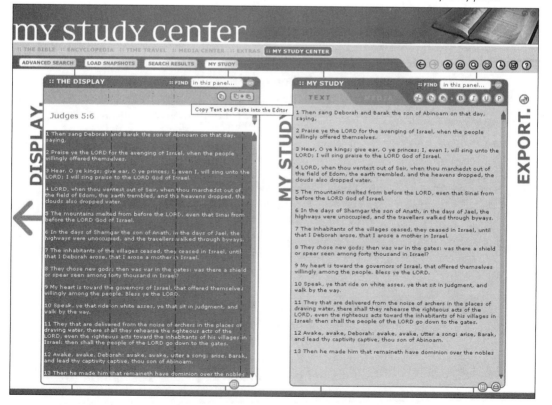

editing. Use the Cut, Copy, and Paste commands within the My Study panel to get the arrangement you want.

PRINTING YOUR EDITED DOCUMENT

When you're finished with your work in the editing space, you can print it or export it. Click the **PRINT** button at the lower right edge of the My Study panel, and a Printer dialog box will pop up—assuming you have a working printer attached to your computer. You tell the printer what it needs to know, and the document will print out as it appears before you on the My Study screen.

Whatever you have on both the Text page and the Media page will be printed.

SAVING YOUR EDITED DOCUMENT TO YOUR COMPUTER

The **EXPORT** button at the right side of the My Study panel allows you to save the document, in its present state, as an .rtf file on your computer. This is Rich Text Format, which practically any word-processing software can read. You will be prompted to select a directory on your computer. Your file will then be saved in the directory you have chosen with the *same name* as the directory you chose.

This will allow you to use the advanced features of other word processors to further enhance the document you create in the My Study panel. The My Study panel is designed for creating personal notes or research files. Anything more complex might need the capabilities of a full-fledged word processing program, which you probably have already! Any of the standard word processors on the market will easily open the .rtf file you create in *iLumina* and take it to the next step.

SAVING MEDIA IMAGES TO YOUR COMPUTER

If the Media page is up front in the My Study panel, you can click the **EXPORT** button at the right side of that panel to save the images you have in My Study Center as .jpg files. This will allow you to open and edit these images in any graphic design software you may own.

BEING LEGAL AND MORAL
IN THE USE OF *ILUMINA* MATERIAL

You are using the information in *iLumina* to create your own study materials. That's the whole idea of My Study Center. But it's important to give credit where credit is due, and not

abuse the resource.

For instance, if you're writing a paper for school, by all means, use *iLumina* as a resource. Quote from it at length, but don't just print out an Encyclopedia article and hand it in as your own work. Yet, if you are creating a new document in which you quote portions of articles from the *iLumina* Encyclopedia or other *iLumina* content, that's not a problem. In a footnote for a paper or book, to give proper credit for a direct quote, you could cite "*iLumina* (Wheaton, IL: Tyndale House, 2003), Encyclopedia, 'Place the name of the article you're quoting here.'"

If you are using whole pages of *iLumina* content, that's a different story. Permission is granted to make up to 50 copies of individual pages for nonprofit noncommercial use, such as handouts for teaching a class. But in those cases, you must put the following credit line at the bottom of each page: From *iLumina,* copyright © 2003 by Tyndale House Publishers, Inc. All rights reserved.

If you are using photographs from *iLumina* in such settings (up to 50 copies, nonprofit, noncommercial), just be sure that the photo credit appears on the page—with one important exception: The photographs with the following

⊕ *The Export dialog box allows you to choose what directory to save My Study Center files and photos in.*

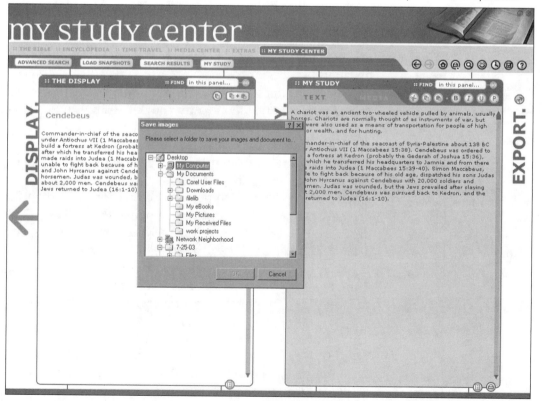

credit line "Preserving Bible Times, Inc. 'Reproduction of the City of Jerusalem at the time of the Second Temple located on the grounds of the Holyland Hotel, Jerusalem'" *must not be reproduced in any way whatsoever.*

In those same settings—up to 50 copies, nonprofit, noncommercial—you may also use maps, charts, Bible studies, and other graphic elements, adapting them for your use. But the credit line must remain visible.

Permission is granted for an instructor to project animations, Virtual Tours, and video clips on a screen for display before an audience for nonprofit noncommercial instructional purposes only. One of the following credit lines should appear at the beginning or at the end of the presentation:

> *Animation from* iLumina *copyright © 2003 by Visual Book Productions. All rights reserved.*

> *Virtual Tour from* iLumina *copyright © 2003 by Visual Book Productions. All rights reserved.*

You may **NOT** reprint groups of pages in bound form, either electronically or physically, or offer copies of printed pages for sale or donation, either at cost or profit. Maps, charts, photographs, Bible studies, and any other graphic element from *iLumina* may **NOT** be placed nor used on websites or intranets.

The King James Version is "public domain," which means you can use that text in any way you'd like. But the New Living Translation (NLT) belongs to Tyndale House Publishers and they state that you may quote as many as 500 verses of the NLT in any form (written, visual, electronic, or audio) without asking special permission from Tyndale House, as long as the verses quoted do not account for more than 25 percent of your work; and you may not quote a whole book of the Bible. (That definitely rules out Obadiah.) And please indicate that the NLT is being quoted.

In any published work quoting the NLT (that is, something being *sold*), one of the following credit lines must appear on the copyright page or title page of the work:

> *Scripture quotations marked NLT are taken from the Holy Bible, New Living Translation, copyright © 1996. Used by permission of Tyndale House Publishers, Inc., Wheaton, Illinois 60189. All rights reserved.*

Here is one special situation: If you're writing a Bible reference book, using the NLT, that's great! Have fun. But you need to ask permission. And quotations in excess of five hundred (500) verses or 25 percent of the work require permission, too. Write to: Tyndale House Publishers, Inc., Attn: Bible Permissions, PO Box 80, Wheaton, IL 60189, or fax in requests to (630) 668-8311. No phone calls please. All requests will be handled in the order received. Please allow 3-4 weeks for a response.

⊕ *My Study Center allows you to save your work and work on it later as well as export it.*

CONTINUING A WORK IN PROGRESS

SAVING A WORK IN PROGRESS

TIP

You will be prompted to save automatically if you leave My Study Center for another part of *iLumina*. It will be there when you come back. But if you exit *iLumina*, lose power, or start a new study, you'll lose any unsaved work. Save often to be safe.

It's good to save your work from time to time, especially if a thunderstorm is approaching. You can save your work in My Study Center by clicking on **MY STUDY** in the Study bar across the top and choosing **SAVE AS** from the submenu that appears. You will be asked to name this study so you can find it later.

LOADING A WORK IN PROGRESS

To reload a My Study Center project that you previously saved, click **LOAD STUDY** on the Study bar. You will then be able to click on any of your saved studies and to load them into the My Study panel.

PART 2

surfing
THE screens ➔

CHAPTER NINE

⊕ THE BIBLE

welcome screen

IF YOU WANT to read or study Scripture, dive in here. This screen offers a number of ways to get into the Bible text and provides access to a host of study resources.

BIBLE VERSION

iLumina Gold has two complete translations of the Bible: the New Living Translation (NLT) and the King James Version (KJV). The NLT is an easy-to-read modern version of the Bible, while the KJV is an older translation. (*iLumina 2.0* has only the NLT.)

In the Pick a Translation area of this screen, clicking on either the **NEW LIVING TRANSLATION** or **KING JAMES VERSION** will take you directly to the Bible text for that translation. Or, if you prefer, you can view both translations at once by clicking on **NLT & KJV SIDE-BY-SIDE**.

BIBLE COMPANIONS

This area contains links to two great sets of Bible exploration tools.

Clicking **BIBLE OVERVIEW** will take you to the Bible Overview screen (see page 111), where you will find complete introductions for every book in the Bible, introductions for both the NLT and KJV, and answers to frequently asked questions about the Bible.

There are also numerous other "Bible Companions" to assist you as you study. These are grouped into four types: Bible notes, Commentaries, Devotional resources, and Study resources. Clicking on any of the specific resources under these headings will take you to that area of the Bible Companions section (see page 103).

HOW DO I GET HERE?
Click THE BIBLE in the menu bar at the top of your screen. (For more on the menu bar, see page 3.)

WHAT'S HERE?
* Bible Version
* Bible Companions
* Bible Resource Index

WHERE CAN I GO FROM HERE?
* Any of the 66 Bible Book Intro screens
* Directly into the Bible text
* Bible Overview page
* Any of the Bible Companions tools

TIP

First-time Bible readers may wish to start with the NLT, since it's a modern English translation—more like reading a newspaper.

⊕ *If you want to read or study the Scripture, dive in at the Bible Welcome screen.*

BIBLE RESOURCE INDEX

The right-hand panel of the Bible Welcome screen contains the Bible Resource Index. Here you can access four additional tools, by clicking your desired resource in the dark blue tab at the left of this panel:

LIST OF BIBLE BOOKS

Click **BIBLE BOOKS** and you'll see a list of all 66 books of the Bible. This functions just like a table of contents for the Bible text. Click on any book name to go to the Bible Book Intro screen (see page 89). Books are listed in the order they appear in most Bibles, but you can choose alphabetical order by clicking the button at the top of the index. Since all 66 books do not fit on your screen, you can use the scroll bar at the right to move the list up and down to find the book you need.

VERSE FINDER

Click **VERSE FINDER** and you'll see a topical index to the Bible. Want to find a verse about faith? Click the plus sign next to Faith in the Verse Finder, and a list of references appears. Click on any one of those references to jump to that passage.

For a somewhat larger sampling, type a word into the search box at the top of the Resource Index window and click the **GO** button. If you type "Faith" there you'll see a list of all the topics that contain the word "Faith."

AN INVITATION TO MEET JESUS

Jesus Christ is at the very core of what the Bible is all about. We hope that as you use *iLumina* to explore the world of the Bible you will develop a deeper and deeper relationship with Jesus Christ. Virtually every tool in *iLumina* can help you develop a fuller understanding of who Jesus is and why you need him in your life. For a concise introduction to Jesus and an explanation of how you can come to know him as your Lord and Savior, click **AN INVITATION TO MEET JESUS**.

TIP

When you are viewing any of the tools available in Additional Resources, you can easily change the current tool by clicking on the drop-down list at the very top of the Bible Resource Index window and selecting a new tool.

ADDITIONAL RESOURCES

Click this and a drop-down menu appears beneath the Bible Resource Index title bar. Click that menu and choose one of the four categories there. Then click a Bible passage to go and read it.

⊕ THE BIBLE
book intro screen

THERE IS A different Book Intro screen for each of the 66 books of the Bible. This is your link to vital information about every Bible book.

BOOK INTRODUCTION

The book introduction appears in the middle of the page. You can make the text of the book introduction larger or smaller by clicking on the text-sizing buttons below this area. (Large T makes it larger, small T smaller, and the text page icon removes search highlighting from the text.)

VITAL STATISTICS

The Vital Statistics section at the left side of your screen gives you important information about the book, such as its author, original audience, and the date it was written. Note that you can jump to certain Encyclopedia articles by clicking on the links in this section.

KEY PLACES

On the right, the Key Places section provides a map and a list of places in the book where most of the main action occurs. Under each place name is a short description telling you why that particular place is important in this book. Some books have more key places than will fit in the space available; if so, move the text up and down by using the scroll bar.

TIMELINE

At the bottom of the screen is a timeline showing the key events of each book in their historical context.

HOW DO I GET HERE?
- Click on a book name in the drop-down list that appears when you click the GO TO button in the Bible toolbar (see page 9).
- Click a link to a Book Intro in any Bible note or Encyclopedia article.

WHAT'S HERE?
- Book Introduction
- Vital Statistics
- Key Places
- Timeline

WHERE CAN I GO FROM HERE?
- Into the Bible text for this book
- To any Encyclopedia articles with links on this page
- To the Bible Atlas

TIP

You can go directly to the beginning of the book by clicking on the GO TO BIBLE BOOK button just below the Book Intro text.

⊕ The Book Intro screens provide vital background information about each book of the Bible.

A Pastor Discovers *iLumina*

They called him Pastor Bob. He'd been preaching just about every week for the last eight years, seven months, and . . . well, who's counting? In the early years of his ministry at Faith Baptist Church, he had been full of fire. Sermons seemed to write themselves. But lately he'd been struggling to come up with something new, something fresh, something right for his congregation. Still, each Sunday the service went on, and he had to step into the pulpit with *something*. He managed, but it was becoming more of a struggle. He remembered the early days when he loved digging out the reference books and researching a sermon. Lately it had become a chore.

Visiting in the home of his Christian education director one day, he caught his first glimpse of *iLumina*. Bob was enthralled as his friend happily showed him through this exciting new program. Bob's wife quietly took note of that and, that Christmas, she bought Bob his own copy of *iLumina Gold*.

He began doing his daily Bible reading on the computer, enjoying the freshness of the New Living Translation. Reading through his favorite book, Romans, he came upon Romans 5:5, a verse he knew well. "And this expectation will not disappoint us. For we know how dearly God loves us, because he has given us the Holy Spirit to fill our hearts with his love." The passage talks about how "problems and trials" develop endurance in us, which develops character, which eventually develops . . . he missed the word *hope* that appears in other translations. He toggled over to the KJV, and sure enough, it said, "Hope maketh not ashamed." Re-reading the NLT, though, he kind of liked the sense of *expectation*. Through our trials, we learn that God helps us, and that gives us an even greater expectation of his ultimate salvation—and it reassures us of his great love.

Bob did a quick search of the word *hope*, zeroing in on several verses in Romans. There it was in Romans 8, as Christians "wait anxiously for that day when God will give us our full rights as his children" (8:23). He always loved that common-sense tag line: "if you already have something, you don't need to hope for it" (8:24).

This was fun! It brought back memories of pawing through dusty concordances in seminary libraries. He used to love all that, but it had become too much work. This computer program, on the other hand, was *easy*. Click a few links and he had all the data he needed. What a fresh, new way to study the Bible!

There was more to this search. As Bob viewed the search results, he saw that the apostle Paul used *hope* again near the end of Romans. Quoting an Isaiah passage that said even the Gentiles would "place their hopes" in the Messiah, Paul prayed that his readers would "overflow with hope through the power of the Holy Spirit" (Romans 15:12-13).

Then Bob noticed the Bible Reference window at the bottom left of his screen. He had the Life Application notes selected, and so he scrolled to the notes on Romans 15:13. "Hope comes as a by-product of the Holy Spirit's work," it said. "It does not come from our own senses or experiences."

Nothing fancy, nothing earth-shaking. But Bob sensed the Spirit saying, "Here it is. Preach on this." Maybe this was the beginning of a new sermon series. As Pastor Bob visualized the faces of his congregation, yes, they definitely needed a word of hope. And maybe he did, too.

➔ THE BIBLE
bible text screen

THE BIBLE TEXT SCREEN is one of the foundations of *iLumina*. Here the Bible will come alive for you as you explore the many media and resource items associated with each chapter of Bible text. This is where you can read God's Word in a refreshing new way!

TEXT AREA

The text area is much more than just a place to read the Bible. You can right-click on any word (Ctrl+click on a Mac) to explore a vast collection of knowledge, special media, photos, and maps. You can also obtain the definition of nearly every word in the Bible and get study helps on every verse. What's more, you can find links to helpful resources like hymns and prayers associated with selected Scripture verses, commentaries, and useful links to the Encyclopedia.

The Bible text that appears in the text area will vary slightly, depending on which Bible version you are viewing. When reading the New Living Translation, you will notice asterisks (*) in the text from time to time. This indicates that there is a special textual note for that verse. (In a printed Bible, these would be footnotes.) Click the asterisk and a text window will appear with the note, generally providing information about translation issues or cross-references.

The text area is similar to a word processor in that you can highlight text and use your mouse or keyboard to copy text to your computer's clipboard. (You can't type your own text in this area, but you *can* in the My Study Center; see page 75). You can even make the text appear larger or smaller by clicking the text-sizing buttons located at the lower right corner of the screen. (Large T makes it larger, small T smaller, and the text page icon removes highlighting .)

The Bible text appears in the text area a chapter at a time.

HOW DO I GET HERE?
- Click the GO TO BIBLE BOOK button on the Book Intro screen (see page 89).
- Type a Bible reference in the GO TO area of the search bar (see page 4).
- Click one of the thousands of Bible references you will find everywhere in *iLumina*.

WHAT'S HERE?
- Text area
- Blueprint Browser
- Media window
- Reference window
- Bible Context menu (appears when you right-click)

WHERE CAN I GO FROM HERE?
- Use the Media window to go to the Media Center.
- Use the Reference window to go to the Bible Companions or the Encyclopedia.
- Click on a map to go to the Bible Atlas.

Since most chapters of the Bible are longer than will fit in the text area, you can move the text up and down using the scroll bar.

BLUEPRINT BROWSER

To help you in navigating through the Bible text, both the New Living Translation and the King James Version are divided into small sections labeled with descriptive headings. By clicking on the Blueprint Browser, you can see a list of the headings available in the book you are currently looking at.

The Blueprint Browser is located just above the text area—it's that bar with two buttons to the left of it and two buttons to the right. If you click on the bar, it expands, and you can see a list of the sections in the book you are reading. Click on any heading to jump to that spot in the text.

Clicking the double arrow on the right will take you to the next *chapter* of the book you are currently reading. The double arrow on the left takes you to the previous chapter. The line-arrow buttons take you to the next or previous *book* of the Bible.

Look up Ecclesiastes 3:1 (NLT) to see that there's a time for everything. Then ALT-click on the "Ecclesiastes" title at the very top right of the screen; you'll go to the place where the *iLumina* creators put in hours and hours of effort— and also had some fun.

MEDIA WINDOW

The Media window is located to the left of the text area, on the upper half of your screen. This is your instant link to hundreds of photos, animations, Virtual Tours, maps, and Points in Time that correspond with the Bible text you are reading. This is where *iLumina* can really make the Bible come alive.

Making media appear in the Media window is easy—you don't have to do anything! Any time you go to a new chapter in the Bible, something visual will automatically appear in the Media window. Every chapter has at least one media element associated with it, and a few chapters have more than one.

There are five types of media available here, and some interesting things you can do with them, using the Media toolbar, just below the media display.

ANIMATIONS

iLumina Gold contains 35 animated Bible stories, and the list keeps growing with every new release. These are professionally developed, cutting-edge digital animations that will entertain and instruct you. When an animation is available for a Bible chapter, the first frame of the animation will automatically appear in the Media window. To play the animation, click the **PLAY** button on the Media toolbar. While the animation is playing, the Play button becomes a **PAUSE** button, which you can click at any time to pause the animation. Clicking on the animation itself will also pause or resume play. Click the **STOP** button to stop playing the animation and return to the beginning. The **PROGRESS SLIDER** gives you an indication of how far along in the animation you are; you can also move the progress slider to any point if you want to start playing the animation from some point other than the beginning. You can change the volume of the animation's soundtrack by clicking the **VOLUME** button. At any point in the animation, you can take a snapshot of the current frame by clicking the **SNAPSHOT** button. Use the **SIZE SELECTOR** to view the animation in full-screen mode or in Theater Mode. At certain times during the animation, you may be able to pause the action and enter into a scene using *iLumina*'s exclusive Point in Time technology (see page 54). When a Point in

⊕ *The Blueprint Browser can help you see the contents of a book quickly.*

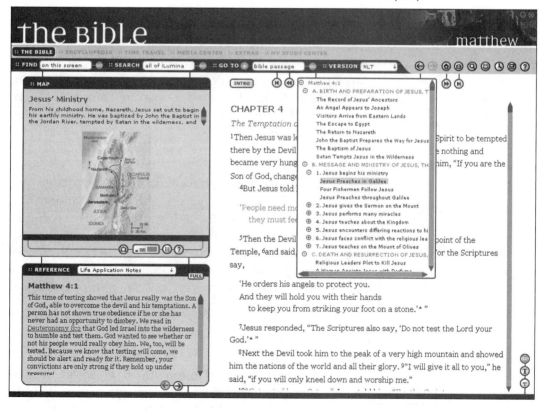

Time is available, the **POINT IN TIME** button will begin flashing. Click this button to jump into the scene and experience the Bible story in a completely new way. Each animation has a title and Scripture, which appear in the caption area. Click the **INDEX** button in the upper right-hand corner of the caption area to go to the Media Center and see an index of all 35 animations.

PHOTOS

Photos are the most common media element, and also the simplest. Each photo has a title and caption associated with it, which you can read in the Media window just above the photo. Use the scroll bar if necessary to view the whole caption. When a photo is displayed, you can click the **SNAPSHOT** button to copy the image to your computer's clipboard. Click the **SIZE** button to view the photo in a larger format or even in Theater Mode. Click the **INDEX** button to go to the Media Center and view a list of all the photos available for the current book of the Bible.

MAPS

Many chapters in the Bible describe a story or some action that takes place in a specific geographic location. These chapters are generally linked to a map, which appears in the Media window, along with a title and caption. When a map is displayed in the Media window, you can take a snapshot with the **SNAPSHOT** button, view the map in Theater Mode, or click the **INDEX** button to view an index of all the maps related to the current Bible book.

VIRTUAL TOUR

Several chapters in the Bible have Virtual Tours associated with them. When a Virtual Tour appears in the Media window, you can interact with it right there. It's just a smaller version of what you would see in the Media Center. Of course you can enlarge the scene by using on the **SIZE SELECTOR** button. Virtual Tours leave the impression that you are actually in the biblical scene. Consult page 40 for tips on navigating through the Virtual Tours.

POINTS IN TIME

Points in Time are frozen scenes from *iLumina*'s animated Bible stories. Ever dreamed of joining the disciples for the Last Supper? Now you can. When a Bible chapter has a Point in

Time associated with it, the scene will automatically appear in the Media window. You can interact with a Point in Time in much the same way that you can interact with a Virtual Tour. (For more on Points in Time, see page 54.) You can enlarge a Point in Time by using the **SIZE SELECTOR**. And you can click the **INDEX** button to go to the Media Center and see a listing of all of *iLumina*'s Points in Time. At any time while you are exploring the scene of a Point in Time, you can jump to the animation and watch the whole story. Do this by clicking on the **POINT IN TIME** button.

REFERENCE WINDOW

The Reference window is your portal to the thousands of study notes, articles, Bible studies, charts, and other resources available in *iLumina*.

Every chapter of the Bible has a default reference article associated with it. Whenever you browse to a new chapter, the default reference item for that chapter will appear in the Reference window. You can change the text in the Reference

⊕ *Some chapters of the Bible, like Exodus 40, have a Point in Time in the Media window.*

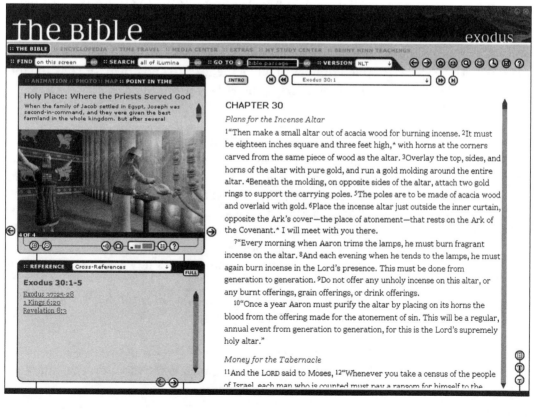

window in four ways. The easiest way is by simply browsing through the Bible. Every time you move to a new chapter, new text appears in the Reference window. Many chapters and verses have more than one possible reference resource available. When this is the case, you can switch back and forth between references by clicking on the title bar of the Reference window, which acts like a drop-down menu. When the menu appears, you can see what other references are available for this chapter or verse. The third way to change the text in the Reference window is to select a new reference resource from the Bible Context menu by right-clicking within any verse or on any word in the text area. (For more on the Bible Context menu, see below.)

If you want to see the content of the Reference window in a broader environment, click the **FULL** button at the upper right. This will take you to the Bible Companions page. (See page 103.)

At the bottom right of the Reference window are two arrow buttons. This is the fourth way to change the text displayed in the window. When you click an arrow button, the Reference window will move to the next (or previous) reference resource associated with the current verse or chapter.

Many of the resources displayed in the Reference window are too long to display all at once. When this is the case, use the scroll bar to move the text up and down, or view the full article by clicking the **FULL** button.

BIBLE CONTEXT MENU

One of the key features of the *iLumina* software is the ability to gain access to a world of information with a single click of your mouse. If you right-click on any word in the text area (Control-click on a Mac), the Bible Context menu will appear on your screen near your mouse pointer. This menu gives you access to the Bible Companion articles, Encyclopedia articles, hymns, prayers, study notes, and other study tools contained in *iLumina*.

The Bible Context menu has four top-level options and five Resource Categories.

TOP-LEVEL OPTIONS:
• Add to Favorites (see page 5 for more on bookmarking and making comments)

SECRET

Look up Ecclesiastes 12:12 (NLT) to see that studying can take forever. Then ALT-click on the "Ecclesiastes" title at the very top right of the screen; you'll go to a place full of books and resources used in creating *iLumina*.

- Copy (to copy selected text to your computer's clipboard)

- Look Up Word (to look up the dictionary definition of any clicked word)

- Search Word (to search all of *iLumina* for other occurrences of the clicked word)

RESOURCE CATEGORIES:

- Bible Notes
  Life Application
  Praise and Worship

- Commentaries
  Comprehensive
  Concise
  Life Application

- Cross-References

- Devotional Resources
  Devotions
  Prayers

⊕ *A drop-down menu will let you select which Bible companion is shown in the Reference window.*

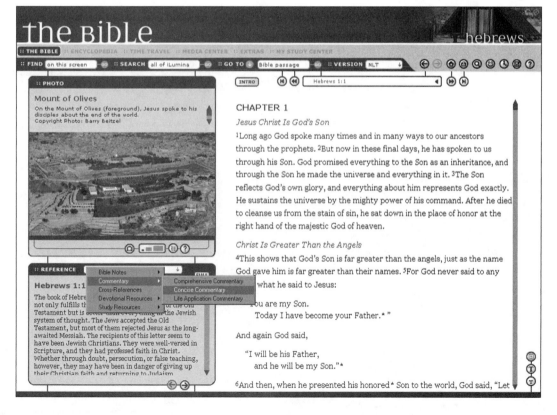

People Profiles on Worship
One Year Reading Plan

- Study Resources
Bible Studies
Charts
Relevant Links
People Profiles on Application
Small Group Discussion Questions

When you hold your mouse over any of the bulleted resource categories, a submenu appears with the options listed below it. Selecting any of these options will display the appropriate text in the Reference window.

For more on the Bible Companions (including the commentaries, Bible notes, reading plan, people profiles, prayers, and devotions), see page 103.

⊛ THE BIBLE
dual translation screen*

IN *ILUMINA GOLD*, you can view the New Living Translation and the King James Version side by side. The options available to you on the Dual Translation screen are virtually identical to those of the Bible text screen (see page 93).

DUAL TRANSLATION TEXT AREA

The Dual Translation text area is located on the right side of your screen, in the same place as the text area on the regular Bible text screen. The Dual Translation area is divided into two sections: the New Living Translation on the left and the King James Version on the right.

As with the Bible text screen, the Bible text is available chapter by chapter. Use the scroll bar to move the text up and down within that chapter. The text of both versions will scroll together so that you can view the same verse in both translations.

The functionality of the Dual Translation area is like that of the Bible text area on the Bible text screen. You can use your mouse to select text, right-click (Control-click on a Mac) on any word or in any verse for further options, and click words with asterisks to view textual notes (see page 93).

BLUEPRINT BROWSER

The Blueprint Browser, located just above the Dual Translation area, works the same way as it does on the regular Bible text screen. Note that when you select a heading in the Blueprint Browser, both translations move to the appropriate verse. But the headings listed in the Blueprint Browser on the Dual Translation screen are the *NLT headings only*. When you click a heading that appears in the NLT but does not appear in

HOW DO I GET HERE?
* Select NLT and KJV from the Version drop-down menu in the Bible toolbar.
* Select NLT and KJV from the Bible Version column on the Bible Welcome screen. (see page 87)
* If you have selected NLT and KJV, you will arrive at this screen every time you click on any Bible link.

WHAT'S HERE?
* Dual-Translation text area
* Blueprint Browser
* Media window
* Reference window
* Bible Context menu

WHERE CAN I GO FROM HERE?
From the Dual Translation page, you can go everywhere you can go from the regular Bible text page.

⊛ *The Dual Translation screen is available in* iLumina Gold.

the KJV or is worded differently in the KJV, the KJV text will still jump to the right verse along with the NLT.

iLumina has only the NLT, not the KJV, so the Dual Translation Screen appears only in *iLumina Gold*.

MEDIA WINDOW AND REFERENCE WINDOW

On the left side of your screen, the Media window appears at the top and the Reference window at the bottom. These work the same way as they do in the regular Bible text screen (see page 93).

BIBLE CONTEXT MENU

Whenever you right-click (Control-click on a Mac) on a word or anywhere in a verse in the Dual Translation area, the Bible Context menu appears—regardless of whether you clicked on the NLT text or the KJV text. Note that you could click in verse 2 in the NLT and get the same menu as if you had clicked in verse 2 in the KJV. The only difference would be if you clicked on a different word. The Bible Context menu is described in more detail on page 98.

⊕ THE BIBLE
bible companions screen

THE BIBLE COMPANIONS screen is a great place to dig into the reference tools *iLumina* offers. There are thousands of Bible study notes, comments on every verse in the Bible, Bible studies, charts, and much, much more. Better than any bookshelf, the Bible Companions can instantly provide the study help or devotional resources you need.

THE COMPANIONS INDEX WINDOW

The Companions Index window is located on the left side of your screen. Here you can access any of the Bible Companions resources. To make things easier, the Bible Companions are broken down into several broad categories, which you can select by clicking on the title bar of the Index window. You'll discover Life Application notes, Praise and Worship notes, as well as Concise, Comprehensive, and Life Application commentaries. Anything you have access to in the Context menu of the Bible text page, you'll find here as well. When you click the title bar, a menu appears displaying the Bible Companions available to you. Pick a Bible Companion, such as Concise Commentary, and an index of all the Concise Commentary notes for the book of Genesis will appear in the index. Simply click the note you wish to view and it will be displayed for you.

Most of these resources are arranged in the order of the books of the Bible. They are commentaries or devotionals that offer notes on the Bible, verse by verse or section by section, so you can call up the notes for, say, John 3:16, by scrolling the index to John, clicking the plus sign, then clicking on chapter 3 or the particular section in which 3:16 falls.

Some of the resources, however, are not keyed in that way to Bible references. These will display indexes of their article titles in alphabetical order. And some of the index lists give you the option of sorting either by Bible book or by article title.

HOW DO I GET HERE?
* Select a Bible Companion in the Bible Context menu on the Bible text screen (see page 93) or the Dual Translation screen (see page 101).
* Click a Bible Companions link on the Bible Welcome screen (see page 87).
* Select one of the BIBLE COMPANIONS from the Bible menu in the *iLumina* menu bar (see page 3).

WHAT'S HERE?
* Companions Index window
* Companions text area
* Bible text Resource window

WHERE CAN I GO FROM HERE?
* Follow any Bible reference link to jump to the Bible text screen.
* Follow any Encyclopedia link to jump to the Encyclopedia.

Most index lists give you the option of narrowing down the list by searching for a key word or phrase. Type a word or phrase into the **FIND** box at the top of the Index window and click the **GO** button. The list will now display only those items whose titles contain the word or phrase you typed. For example, if you're looking at the Devotions index, and you want to see a list of devotions with titles that contain the word "love," type the word "love" in the **FIND** box and click **GO**. Now the only items in the index list are devotions with titles that contain the word "love."

Once you navigate the index to find what you want, click on it, and the corresponding text will appear in the Companions text area.

Here's a brief description of the Bible Companions available in *iLumina Gold*.

BIBLE NOTES

Life Application Study Notes

Originally published as part of the best-selling *Life Application Study Bible*, the Life Application study notes provide helpful details on many verses in the Bible.

Praise and Worship Study Notes

From the *Praise and Worship Study Bible*, these study notes provide insight on how people and events in the Bible are related to the consistent pursuit of a life dedicated to praising God.

COMMENTARY

Comprehensive Commentary

The Comprehensive Commentary notes are from the *New Commentary on the Whole Bible*, Old Testament and New Testament volumes. This classic commentary is based mainly on the text of the King James Version and offers helpful insights on nearly every verse in Scripture.

Concise Commentary

The Concise Commentary offers helpful comments on larger chunks of the Bible text. This is a great resource for people interested in gaining a better understanding of how the whole Bible fits together.

Life Application Commentary

These commentary notes first appeared in the popular Life Application Commentary series and cover only the New Testament. With a focus on how the Bible text can be applied to everyday life, this commentary is extremely useful for small-groups or Sunday school classes, or for personal devotions.

CROSS-REFERENCES

Cross-references are other Bible verses that relate in some way to the text you've selected. Perhaps the New Testament quotes an Old Testament verse or alludes to an Old Testament story. Maybe there's a theme introduced in one verse that another verse develops. In any case, your study of one passage might be enhanced by a look at another.

DEVOTIONAL RESOURCES

Devotions
365 insightful devotions from *One Year through the Bible* linked to the Scripture text of each devotion.

Prayers
These inspirational and historic prayers designed to help you pray through the Scriptures are taken from the *Praise and Worship Study Bible.*

⊕ *The commentaries available on the Bible Companion screen are indexed by book, chapter, and verse.*

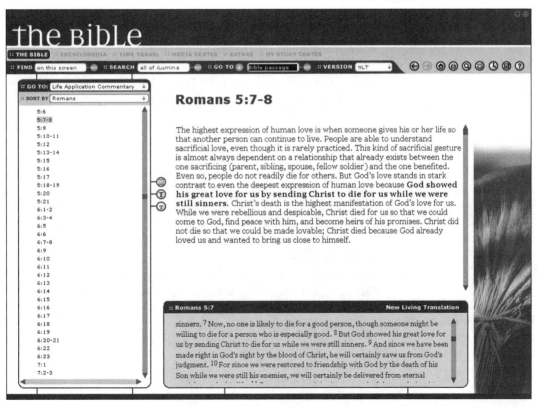

Praise and Worship Profiles

These profiles of biblical people are from the *Praise and Worship Study Bible*. Not only will you learn about major personalities in the Bible, you'll get a unique perspective on the place of worship in their lives.

One Year Reading Plan

The One Year Bible is one of the most popular ways to read through the entire Bible in a single year. Now you can utilize the same easy reading plan by using *iLumina* to read through the Bible in a year.

STUDY RESOURCES

Bible Charts

iLumina has numerous charts available to enhance your Bible study. For the most convenient viewing and printing, we've installed them as .pdf files, viewable through the Adobe Reader technology which is integrated into the Charts and Bible Studies screen. Choose this option to browse the charts.

Bible Studies

You can also access all the *Life Application Bible* study guides for the New Testament to assist you with studying any New Testament passage, whether you're leading a group or just studying on your own. Selecting this option will take you to the Charts and Bible Studies screen. Like the Charts, the Bible Studies are stored as .pdf files, viewable through Adobe Reader technology.

Life Application Profiles

The Bible is full of wonderful stories about people like us. One of the most inspiring features of the *Life Application Bible* has been its character profiles, which focus on Bible characters such as Ruth, David, Mary, and Paul. We're pleased to include these profiles as Bible Companions.

Relevant Links

In your Bible study, you will run across themes you want to know more about. So among the Bible Companions we include links to the *iLumina* Encyclopedia. Clicking here will take you to the Encyclopedia section, but you can also come back via the Back button or the History button in the toolbar.

Small Group Discussion Questions

This is just one of *iLumina*'s great resources for small group

SECRET

Look up Proverbs 16:9 (NLT) to see how important our plans are. Then ALT-click on the "Proverbs" title at the very top right of the screen; you'll go to a place where the makers of *iLumina* were constantly reminded of the truth of that verse.

leaders: questions for reflection and discussion. *iLumina* has questions designed to start discussion and probe into key ideas for every chapter of the Bible.

COMPANIONS TEXT AREA

In the center of your screen is the Companions text area. When you click on different items in the Companions Index, the text of the reference resource you have selected will appear here. This area may contain links to the Bible text which will take you to that passage in The Bible section of *iLumina*. As with the Bible text area on the Bible text screen, you can right-click (Control-click on a Mac) on any word to get the dictionary definition of that word.

BIBLE TEXT RESOURCE WINDOW

The Bible text Resource window, located below the Companions text area, is a scrollable window that allows you to follow along in the Bible text as you are studying any of the many reference resources available to you in *iLumina*.

© *Life Application Profiles give lessons from the lives of well-known biblical characters.*

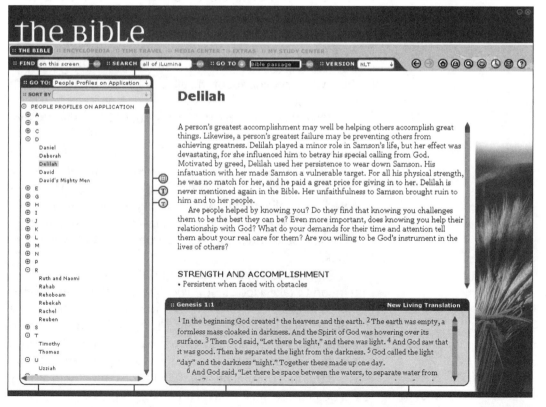

Questions for a Bible Study Leader

When Carol was first asked to lead the Thursday night women's Bible study, it was a temporary thing, six weeks at the most. She was scared silly, but she agreed to do it. That was two years ago. She hasn't stopped since.

At first she worried that she didn't know enough about the Bible. She still feels insecure about that, but she soon learned that leading a Bible study group like this was more about asking questions than giving answers. She didn't have to impart information; she just had to guide the group as they dug into Scripture together. Carol found that she was actually pretty good at listening to people's comments and focusing a discussion on the main themes of a Bible text.

Over her two-year tenure leading this group, they had used a number of different Bible study guides. Some were more helpful than others. Carol didn't like the ones that did more teaching than questioning. The women in her group were pretty good at coming up with multiple answers to well-worded, open-ended questions. But when a study guide told them what to think about the Bible, they didn't have so much to talk about.

When they decided to tackle the book of Ephesians, someone suggested a new study guide, and they tried it for a few sessions, but frankly it wasn't very helpful. They decided to ditch it. But then what? The church had already bought those booklets for the group, and there was nothing more budgeted. Rachelle mentioned that her family had recently bought this great *iLumina* program, and she thought there were Bible study guides in there. She invited Carol over to take a look.

So Carol stopped over at Rachelle's place that Sunday afternoon to take a look at *iLumina*. She almost missed the evening church service, she was so enthralled. Yes, there were Bible study guides for every New Testament book, including Ephesians. There were also charts that could be printed out. Not to mention photos, maps, and background articles. This was a treasure trove of helpful stuff. It would give them all they needed for the Bible study, and more.

The study guide pages had questions—good, thoughtful questions—but they left room for reflection and discussion. When background was necessary, it was provided, and Carol (once she got her own copy) loved to scour the rest of *iLumina* for additional background info she could bring to the group. Besides the seven study-guide lessons on Ephesians, there were nearly a dozen charts on various issues from Ephesians. Carol didn't want to overwhelm the group with handouts, but she picked out three or four charts that would be especially helpful. She also searched the Photos Index for pictures of Ephesus. With help from her camera-buff son, she was able to print these out on photo paper and bring a mini-album to the group.

Now when they read the background story of Paul's experiences in Ephesus in Acts 19, where the worshipers of the goddess Artemis start a riot and assemble in the amphitheater, *they could see pictures of that very amphitheater and a nearby temple of Artemis*. They could see the impressive remains of first-century building projects—*the same buildings Paul's original readers would have had in mind*—as they read Ephesians 2:20-21: "We are his house, built on the foundation of the apostles and the prophets. And the cornerstone is Christ Jesus himself. We who believe are carefully joined together, becoming a holy temple for the Lord."

The Thursday night Bible study group was never at a loss for words, but this fresh material added a new degree of meaning to their discussions.

⊕ THE BIBLE
bible overview screen

THE BIBLE OVERVIEW screen is your one-stop resource for a wealth of information about every book in the Bible, the different Bible versions available in *iLumina*, and answers to questions about the Bible as a whole.

REFERENCE INDEX WINDOW

At the left side of your screen, the Reference Index window lists the resources available on this screen. At any time, it will display one of three lists: Bible Book Overviews, Version Introductions, or Questions about the Bible. You can change the current list by clicking the title bar of this window and selecting another list in the drop-down menu.

BIBLE BOOK OVERVIEWS

Bible Book Overviews are a simple way to gain in-depth information about each book of the Bible. This reference is displayed as a list of the books of the Bible. Scroll up or down as necessary to select the book you want to know more about, and click on the plus sign next to its name. That will unfurl a list of four or five resources, which you can click on.

Clicking the **IN BRIEF** link brings a short description of the book and its major themes up in the Overview text area. The other links bring up introductions to the book from various commentaries, each with a different emphasis.

The **CONCISE INTRODUCTION** focuses on the book as a whole. The **COMMENTARY INTRODUCTION** gives background information on the book and provides insight on how this book relates to other books. The **PRAISE AND WORSHIP INTRODUCTION** provides special emphasis on the worship-related aspects of the book. For New Testament books only, the **APPLICATION INTRODUCTION** provides insight on how you can apply the book's themes to your own life.

HOW DO I GET HERE?
• Click on one of the links beneath Bible Companions on the Bible Welcome screen: Bible Overviews, Questions About the Bible, or Version Introductions (see page 20).
• Click on BIBLE OVERVIEWS in the drop-down Bible menu in the *iLumina* menu bar (for more on the *iLumina* menu bar, see page 3).

WHAT'S HERE?
• Reference Index window
• Overview text area

WHERE CAN I GO FROM HERE?
• Jump to Bible verses from links in the overview text.
• Jump to Encyclopedia articles from links in the overview text.

⊕ *The Bible Overview screen provides multiple introductions for each book.*

VERSION INTRODUCTIONS

This selection allows you to read the introductions for the Bible versions used in *iLumina*. You can read the translators' introduction to the New Living Translation and the original dedicatory epistle to the King James Version. These introductions can give you insight into the nature of each translation and how each can best be used in your studies.

In addition, you can see the introductions to some of the other Bible resources available to you in *iLumina*, such as the Life Application Study notes and the Praise and Worship Study notes.

To view an introduction, click on its title in the Reference window, and the text of the introduction will appear in the Overview text window.

QUESTIONS ABOUT THE BIBLE

From this list, you can find answers to many of the most frequently asked questions about the Bible. Simply click on any question, and text of the answer will appear in the Overview text area.

OVERVIEW TEXT AREA

The Overview text area in the center of your screen is where you can view information after clicking on resource items in the Reference Index window.

As in other text windows, you can use the scroll bar to move the text up and down if necessary. Make the text larger or smaller by clicking on the text-resizing buttons to the left of the Overview text area. To return the text to its original size, you can either reload the article by clicking its title again in the Index window or click **BACK** and then **FORWARD** on the *iLumina* toolbar.

⊙ THE BIBLE
charts and bible studies

ILUMINA HAS HUNDREDS of charts and Bible studies, which you can view here. With the sorting and searching capabilities of the Index window, you can quickly find the chart or Bible study you need.

INDEX WINDOW

At the left side of your screen, the Index window contains a list of all the charts and Bible studies contained in *iLumina*. To toggle between charts and Bible studies, click the title bar of the Index window, which functions as a drop-down menu. Click the index you want to view.

The charts and Bible studies are organized by Bible book. To see the charts or Bible studies available for any book, simply click on the book's name in the Index window. Then click on any item in the list that emerges, and the appropriate chart or Bible study will appear in the Viewer window.

To narrow the index a bit, you can type any word or phrase into the **FIND** box at the top of the Index window. When you click the **GO** button, the list of charts or Bible studies reforms to display only the items whose titles contain the word or phrase you typed. For example, if you want a list of charts with titles containing the name Jesus, type "Jesus" into the Find text box and click **GO**. Now the Index window contains only charts with the word "Jesus" in the title.

VIEWER WINDOW

The Viewer window is the right-hand portion of the screen. This is the area where the charts and Bible studies will appear when you click a title in the Index window. Here, *iLumina* uses Adobe's Page Display Format (also referred to as *.pdf*

HOW DO I GET HERE?
• Click on a chart or Bible study link in the Bible Context menu which appears in the Bible text screen.
• Click on the CHARTS AND BIBLE STUDIES link on the Bible Overview screen.
• Select CHARTS AND BIBLE STUDIES from the drop-down menu on the Bible Overview screen.

WHAT'S HERE?
• Index window
• Viewer window

WHERE CAN I GO FROM HERE?
From here there's no direct link forward. You can go back where you came from (with either the Back or History button on the toolbar), or use the menu bar to enter any new section of *iLumina*.

files), which allows you to view the contents of a page exactly the same way it originally appeared on paper. This format is well suited for charts and Bible studies.

So, when you call up a chart or Bible study, *iLumina* automatically loads and runs Adobe Reader within the Viewer window (it may take a few extra seconds to load). The Search and Print functions of *iLumina* won't work with these documents, but Adobe Reader has its own toolbar with similar functions. That toolbar appears just below the title bar of the Viewer window.

The leftmost button on the Adobe Reader's toolbar is the **SAVE** button. Click this button to save the chart or Bible study you are currently viewing to a specific location on your computer's hard drive. Next to the Save button is the **PRINT** button, which will print the chart or Bible study only, and not the Index window or the rest of your screen. Two buttons to the right is the **SEARCH** button (it looks like a set of binoculars), which you can use to find text within the chart or Bible study.

Some charts or Bible studies may be too big to completely fit in the Viewer window. When this is the case, you can use the scroll bars to move the document up and down or left and right. You can also move the document by clicking directly on the Viewer window and dragging the image. (Dragging will only work when the mouse pointer looks like a little hand. If it doesn't, click the button with the hand icon in the toolbar.)

At the right of the toolbar are the selection tools, which you can use to select text or graphics and copy them into another program, such as a word processor or a graphics editor. The button that looks like an uppercase T with a little square is the **TEXT-SELECT** tool. After you click this button, you can select text in the document and copy it by pressing CTRL+C or clicking the **COPY** button in the toolbar (next to the **PRINT** button). Next to the text-select button is the **GRAPH-ICS-SELECT** button. After you click this button, you can use your mouse to draw a box around any portion of the document. Pressing CTRL+C or clicking the **COPY** button will copy whatever is in the box onto your computer's clipboard as an image, which you can then paste into any graphics editing program.

If the .pdf document looks too big or too small, you can resize it with the **ZOOM** button, which looks like a magnifying glass with a small plus symbol (+) on it. Click this button,

TIP

For more information about viewing *.pdf* files with Adobe Reader, see the Adobe Help system, available on Adobe's toolbar.

then click on the document to make the text bigger. Notice the small arrow to the immediate right of the Zoom button. If you click this arrow, you can select whether you want to zoom in or zoom out. You can also control the zoom by typing a percentage into the Zoom text box at the bottom left of the toolbar.

⊕ *Bible Charts and Studies are displayed in .pdf format using Adobe Reader.*

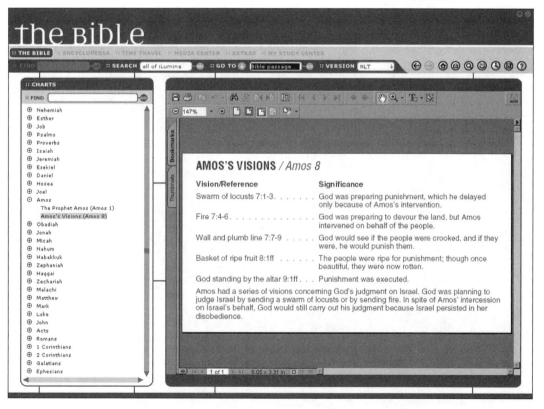

CHAPTER TEN

⊖ ENCYCLOPEDIA
welcome screen

THIS IS YOUR entry point into the amazing *iLumina* Encyclopedia, containing about 8,900 articles with information about virtually any Bible topic you can think of, a complete Bible Dictionary, as well as overviews of Christian doctrine and theology, biographies of historical Christians, and much, much more. Whether you're studying for a test, writing a paper, preparing a sermon, or just interested in learning more about the Bible, this is the place to start.

HOW DO I GET HERE?
By clicking on ENCYCLOPEDIA in the menu bar (see page 3).

WHAT'S HERE?
Links to Encyclopedia focus areas

WHERE CAN I GO FROM HERE?
Any of the Encyclopedia focus areas available in your version of *iLumina*

ENCYCLOPEDIA FOCUS AREAS

iLumina's Encyclopedia has thousands of articles, divided into four focus areas: Top Topics, Bible Dictionary, Life Application, and Christian History. With *iLumina Gold*, you have access to three more Encyclopedia focus areas. The areas available to you are listed (or pictured) on this Encyclopedia Welcome screen.

To access a list of articles in any focus area, simply click on its picture or name. You can also view an extended list of all the articles in the *iLumina* Encyclopedia by clicking on **ALL ARTICLES**.

⊕ *The Encyclopedia Welcome screen lets you jump to any of the available focus areas.*

TOP TOPICS

iLumina contains 100 Top Topics articles (*iLumina Gold* contains even more), specially designed to give you a complete multimedia experience. These articles contain photos, maps, and extensive links to Scripture verses and other Encyclopedia articles. Some Top Topics articles contain animation, virtual tours, or Points in Time.

BIBLE DICTIONARY

With over 5,000 articles, the Bible Dictionary has articles about every person, place, and event in the Bible. It contains information about every plant and animal in the Bible, cultural and historical issues of Bible times, and key biblical themes.

LIFE APPLICATION
"So what?" That's the underlying question in the nearly 1,000 articles in this focus area, designed to help you put Scripture's teaching into practice with helpful links and key verses for memorization.

CHRISTIAN HISTORY
iLumina includes nearly 1,500 articles about key people in the history of Christianity. *iLumina Gold* adds articles on events, movements and key books in Christian history.

The following focus areas are only available in *iLumina Gold:*

THEOLOGY*
You'll find hundreds of articles on major topics of Christian doctrine. The Theology focus area includes definitions of key terms, Scripture passages that are often quoted in everyday life and topics about the Bible that every Christian should know.

HYMNS*
The Hymns focus area contains the lyrics of several hundred traditional hymns, along with devotional comments to help you gain a better understanding of what these hymns mean, who wrote them, and how they can help you gain a richer understanding of God and his Word. Selected hymns even have an audio rendition of the melody.

DEUTERO-CANONICAL BOOKS*
Also known as the Apocrypha, these inter-Testamental books are accepted as Holy Scripture by the Roman Catholic Church, but absent from most Bibles used by Protestants. The text of these books is included here to give Protestant users a broader understanding of biblical history and to give Catholic users a complete version of the Bible as they are used to seeing it.

A Music Director Hunts for Hymns

Every Tuesday the pastor told Marian what he would preach on the following Sunday. In her role as music director, she would then select appropriate hymns for the small congregation to sing. She believed that music often complemented good preaching by providing an emotional context. A sermon about joy could instruct the mind, but the singing of "Joyful, Joyful We Adore Thee" would certainly stir joy in the soul. And so she prided herself on finding the perfect hymns to assist the pastor's preaching ministry.

One Tuesday, however, Marian didn't get word of the pastor's topic. She called him on Wednesday and left a message. He e-mailed her Thursday, saying he was still wrestling with it. She responded, humbly expressing her inner thoughts, *Wrestle away! But the bulletin goes to the printer at 10 A.M. Friday and I need hymn numbers.*

The pastor called her, apologetically at 9:15 A.M. Friday, saying he had finally decided. The Lord was leading him to preach about Enoch.

Enoch.

She wanted to ask him if he was sure he heard the Lord correctly, but she knew the pastor had already given his message serious and prayerful consideration and there really was no time left for discussion anyway, so she kept quiet. She tried again to think of any hymns that had been written based on the life of Enoch. As you might guess, she drew a blank.

It was already past 9:30 when she desperately clicked the *iLumina* icon on her computer. First she loaded the Bible section and searched for Enoch. The main story was in Genesis 5:24—"He enjoyed a close relationship with God throughout his life. Then suddenly, he disappeared because God took him." That was all. She clicked over to the KJV translation— "Enoch walked with God: and he was not; for God took him." She appreciated both the simplicity of the modern text and the mysterious poetry of the Elizabethan English. But she still had a job to do.

Walk! She thought. Aren't there hymns about walking with God? She knew right where to go. Clicking over to the Encyclo- ⊕ PAGE 119 pedia section, she clicked on Hymns. Then she did a search for "walk."

"Just a Closer Walk with Thee." *Of course! The old spiritual! That's one. I need one more.*

"O Master, Let Me Walk with Thee." Unfortunately, Marian couldn't find that one in the church's hymnal.

"O for a Closer Walk with God." She didn't know this hymn, but she knew the lyricist, William Cowper, had written several other hymns. She was relieved to find this one in the hymnal. And then she read more of what *iLumina* had to say about this song.

Cowper struggled with psychological problems throughout his life, and had to be hospitalized several times for insanity. A healing force in his life was his friendship with John Newton, best known as the writer of "Amazing Grace." The two men took long walks together, telling jokes and talking poetry. That background gave a deeper meaning to the last stanza of this hymn:

So shall my walk be close with God,
Calm and serene my frame;
So purer light shall mark the road
That leads me to the Lamb.

Marian decided she would introduce the hymn by saying a few things about William Cowper. She was overjoyed to discover, in *iLumina*'s hymn section, that this hymn text was written after Cowper read about Enoch in Genesis 5:24. Marian was relieved. The bulletin would make its 10 o'clock deadline, complete with hymns about Enoch.

⊕ ENCYCLOPEDIA
encyclopedia entry screen

THE ENCYCLOPEDIA is one of the most exciting and useful features in all of *iLumina*. Packed with information, the thousands of articles and informational resources here will assist you with creating projects and reports, help you learn about Christian history or theology, or just give you interesting stuff to read.

ARTICLE INDEX WINDOW

The Article Index window along the left side of the screen lets you access the thousands of articles in the *iLumina* Encyclopedia. When you select a particular focus area, the articles in that focus area will be listed here. Click on the name of any article to load the text of that article into the Encyclopedia text area.

At any time you can change the focus area listed by clicking on the title bar of the Article Index window. A menu will drop down with the names of all available focus areas. Click on one to switch to that listing.

Larger lists are arranged by letter. In these cases, a Letter menu appears under the title bar of this window. Click on the first letter of the subject you're looking up, and all articles beginning with that letter will be listed. You could also type your target subject into the **FIND** text box at the top of this window. Every letter you type into that box will narrow down the list, until you find your subject. (If you type a letter combination that does not match the title of any article, the list will disappear altogether.)

As with any list or article in *iLumina,* if an index is too long for the window, use the scroll bar at the right to move up or down.

ENCYCLOPEDIA TEXT AREA

Whenever you click on an article title in the Article Index window, the text of Encyclopedia articles will appear in the

HOW DO I GET HERE?
- Click a link to an Encyclopedia article anywhere in *iLumina.*
- Click the name of an Encyclopedia focus area on the Encyclopedia Welcome screen.
- Click an Encyclopedia article link anywhere in *iLumina.*
- Click ENCYCLOPEDIA on the *iLumina* menu bar, and click the name of a focus area in the drop-down menu.

WHAT'S HERE?
- Article Index window
- Encyclopedia text area
- Media Resource window (for some articles)
- Reference window (for some articles)

WHERE CAN I GO FROM HERE?
- Jump to the Bible by clicking a Bible reference link.
- Jump to another Encyclopedia article by clicking an article link.
- Go to the Bible Atlas by clicking on a map.
- Go to the Media Center by clicking the Index button in the Media Resource window.

middle of your screen. (When you click on any Encyclopedia link in *iLumina*, this screen will appear with the text of that article already in place, in this text area.) Use the scroll bar as necessary to move up or down within the article.

Some articles are very short, only a few sentences or even just a few words; others are much longer. Some are divided by headings, which you can browse using the Article Outline in the Reference window (see below). Just click on any point in the outline to jump to that point in the article.

Some articles have photos or maps or other media linked to them. When you are viewing one of these articles, you will see the Media Resource window to the right of the text area. When you are looking at an article that does not contain any media links, the Media Resource window will not be visible.

If the type is too big or too small for you to read comfortably, use the text-sizing buttons to change the appearance of the text. These are left of the text area, beside the Article Index window. Click the large T to make the text bigger, the small T to shrink it, and the topmost button to remove highlighting from the text.

MEDIA RESOURCE WINDOW

Many articles in the *iLumina* Encyclopedia contain special media resources, such as photos, maps, or Virtual Tours. In these cases, the Media Resource window will appear to the right of the text area and above the Reference window.

At the top of the window, the Media Chooser bar lists the various media options available for the article you are currently viewing. Many times only one option will appear in the Chooser bar, but some articles will have more than one kind of media for you to select from. The possible media types are Animations, Photos, Maps, and Virtual Tours. Click on the media type you want to view, and it will appear in the Media window. For example, if the article you are looking at contains photos, you can click **PHOTOS** in the Media Chooser bar. Then, if more than one photo is available, you can click the arrows that appear just outside the lower left and right corners of the Photo to flip through the available pictures.

Just above the media you're viewing, a caption area displays the title of the media element along with a short description if one is available. Most maps, for example, contain a short caption that describes the significance of the map. Copyright information for photos may also be displayed in this area. If the text of the caption is too long to fit in the caption area all at once, you can use the scroll bar to move the text up and down. The button in the caption area turns off the caption if you find the text scrolling in this window distracting while watching the digital animation or video in the Media window.

The Media area is the main part of the Media Resource window, where the media element you have selected is actually displayed. Click on a photo to go to the Media Center and view an index of all the hundreds of photos in *iLumina*. Click on a map to go to the Bible Atlas and check out other maps. If a Virtual Tour is displayed, you can move the picture around right in the Media window, just as you do in the Virtual Tour area of the Media Center (see page 139).

The Media toolbar at the bottom of the Media Resource window gives you the tools you need with various media. If you are viewing an animation, you can use the **PLAY/PAUSE** and **STOP** buttons to start and stop the animation. The **PROGRESS SLIDER** shows you how far along you are in the animation—you can also drag it to view the animation from

⊕ *For some articles, the media window will appear on the right displaying a picture or map.*

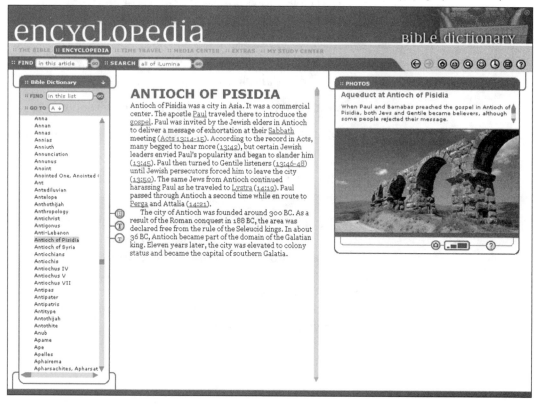

any point. Click the **VOLUME** button to find a comfortable listening level. Next is the **SNAPSHOT** button, which you can click to capture a copy of a photo, map, or animation frame to your computer's clipboard. You can then paste the image into a graphics editing program. The **SIZE SELECTOR** toggles the display size of the media from small to large to Theater Mode (see page 59). Beside that is the **HELP** button. At the far right of the Media toolbar, the **POINT IN TIME** button will appear with some animations or Virtual Tours. When this is blinking, click on it to enter the biblical story.

TIP

Even in this Media window, animations start up automatically, so you might not be ready for them. Click the STOP button to reset it to play from the beginning. You can also click right on the animation itself to pause a playing animation or to play a paused one.

REFERENCE WINDOW

The articles in the Top Topics focus area contain additional reference resources, which appears at the bottom-right corner of the screen in a Reference window. (If you're looking at an article that does not contain any additional references, the Reference window is not visible.)

Any of six resources might show up in the Reference window:

- **OUTLINE** shows a hierarchical list of all the headings in the current article. Click on any heading to jump to that spot in the article.

- **FAST FACTS** give you a quick who-what-when-where-why of the article topic.

- **WACKY WIT** offers a creative take on the subject.

- **DIGGING DEEPER** lists links to some study themes connected to the subject.

- **LIFE LINKS** gives a list of life-issue links related to the main subject.

- **PEOPLE PROFILES** presents a list of other biblical or historical figures you might want to explore. Click on any of these links to read those Encyclopedia articles.

Click on the title bar of the Reference window to see which resources are available, and click on any resource type in the drop-down menu to select it.

CHAPTER ELEVEN

⊖ TIME TRAVEL
welcome screen

PEOPLE OFTEN *KNOW* Bible stories, but they're not sure where they land. And they might know a few details of the early church or the Reformation, but there are lots of gaps. Was David before or after Daniel? Did John Calvin precede Martin Luther? And where do Bible stories fit into the history of Egypt, Greece, or Rome? *iLumina*'s Time Travel feature allows you to see the spread of human history. Here you can fill in the gaps and fit the pieces together.

HOW DO I GET HERE?
Click TIME TRAVEL on the menu bar, and then click INTRO on the drop-down menu.

WHAT'S HERE?
Time Travel Era Browser

WHERE CAN I GO FROM HERE?
Any of the 14 Time Travel Eras

TIME TRAVEL ERA BROWSER

The 14 Time Travel eras span all of history from Creation to today. Move your mouse across the pictures, and you'll see time passing in front of you. Each picture stands for one of the 14 eras, so the title in the center of the screen will change as your mouse moves from one image to the next. Click on one of the pictures to take a look at the era it represents.

These are the 14 eras you can choose from.

⊕iLumina *gives you 14 eras to choose from in the Time Travel section.*

- **BEGINNINGS** covers Creation through the period of the Patriarchs (?–1876 B.C.).

- **SLAVERY TO SETTLEMENT** covers the 400 years of Israelite slavery in Egypt through the settlement of the Promised Land (1876–1375 B.C.).

- **JUDGES AND KINGS** covers the period of the judges through the reign of Solomon (1375–930 B.C.).

- **THE DIVIDED KINGDOM** covers the division of Israel and Judah after Solomon through the destruction of Jerusalem by Babylon (930–586 B.C.).

- **EXILE, RETURN, AND INDEPENDENCE** covers Jewish

history from the Exile through the inter-Testamental period up to the reign of Herod the Great (586–6 B.C.).

• **JESUS' LIFE AND MINISTRY** covers the earthly ministry of Jesus Christ from his birth to his crucifixion, resurrection, and ascension (6 B.C.–A.D. 30).

• **THE EARLIEST CHURCH** covers the giving of the Holy Spirit at Pentecost through the apostle John's exile on the island of Patmos (A.D. 30–100).

• **THE CHURCH IN THE PAGAN ROMAN EMPIRE** covers the death of the apostle John through the persecution of Christians under Emperor Diocletian of Rome (A.D. 100–312).

• **THE AGE OF THE CHRISTIAN ROMAN EMPIRE** covers the conversion of Emperor Constantine through the later church fathers, into the Middle Ages (312–800).

• **THE HOLY ROMAN EMPIRE** covers the reign of Charlemagne to the beginnings of the Reformation (800–1517).

• **THE REFORMATION** covers church history from Martin Luther's *Ninety-Five Theses* through the Pilgrims' landing at Plymouth Rock (1517–1648).

• **THE AGE OF REASON AND REVIVAL** covers the establishment of the Quakers through the Great Awakening to the establishment of Sunday school (1648–1789).

• **AN ERA OF MISSIONS AND DENOMINATIONS** covers the abolition of slavery in Britain through the beginning of the Pentecostal and Fundamentalist movements (1789–1914).

• **A TIME OF CONFLICT AND TECHNOLOGY** covers the first Christian radio broadcast through recent events (1914 to the present).

⊕ TIME TRAVEL
time travel era screen

The major events of each era are listed, with Spotlights on some that deserve more attention.

MAIN TIMELINE AREA

The Main Timeline area is the large area in the center-left of the screen. There are basically two things you can do in this area (besides reading and enriching your knowledge of history). You can click on any of five different kinds of links, and you can drag the timeline back and forth through history.

The five kinds of links you can click on in the Main Timeline area are:

- **BIBLE LINKS** (which take you to Bible verses)

- **ENCYCLOPEDIA LINKS** (which take you to Encyclopedia articles)

- **ANIMATION LINKS** (which take you to the Media Center Animations page)

- **VIRTUAL TOUR LINKS** (which take you to the Media Center Virtual Tours page)

- **SPOTLIGHT LINKS**, which make new content appear in the Spotlight window (see below).

Dragging the Timeline is a great way to see history unfolding before your eyes. Just click anywhere on the timeline and hold the clicker down as you move your mouse right or left. (But don't click on any link, or you'll be taken somewhere else as soon as you release your mouse.)

HOW DO I GET HERE?
Click on any of the era-stripes on the Time Travel Welcome screen (see page 125).

WHAT'S HERE?
- Main Timeline area
- Master Timeline
- Title area
- Spotlight window
- Other Happenings

WHERE CAN I GO FROM HERE?
- Jump to the Bible with hundreds of Bible links.
- Jump to the Encyclopedia with dozens of links to Encyclopedia articles.
- Jump to the Media Center for a larger view of dozens of photographs, animations, and Virtual Tours.

MASTER TIMELINE

The Master Timeline appears at the top of the screen above the Main Timeline area and just below the Title, spanning all of history. As you make your way through history in the Main Timeline area, you'll notice that a bold line segment appears on the Master Timeline in the area corresponding to the dates of the era you are in.

You can jump immediately to any point in history by clicking on that point in the Master Timeline. You can also navigate era by era by clicking the arrows at the extreme left and right of the Master Timeline. These will move you to the next era or to the previous one.

TITLE AREA

As you move from era to era, in the Title area, just above the Master Timeline, you'll see the title and dates of the era you're in.

SPOTLIGHT WINDOW

The Spotlight window, along the right side of the screen, displays in-depth information about certain people and events in history. One person or event is automatically spotlighted when you arrive in any era, but you can change the contents of the Spotlight window by clicking on any other Spotlight link in the Main Timeline area. The Spotlight links are the square pictures attached to some events, generally three or four per era. (Don't confuse the Spotlight links with the Animation links, which are smaller and rectangular.)

When you click a Spotlight link, two things happen. First, the picture from the link appears in the larger image area at the top of the Spotlight window. Second, a list of important dates related to the featured person or event appear under the picture. Use the scroll bar to move through the entire text of the Spotlight.

Many Spotlights contain links to Bible verses or Encyclopedia articles in the text. Click on any link to jump to that spot and read related content.

OTHER HAPPENINGS

The Other Happenings window appears at the bottom of the screen. Each era has a distinct collection of information in this window, grouped in six categories:

- **TECHNOLOGY**—what was being invented around the world?

- **WORLD POWER**—who were the big dogs in world politics during this era?

- **CULTURE**—what major cultural events or changes were taking place?

- **RELIGION AND PHILOSOPHY**—what new religious movements were appearing?

- **BEYOND THE (MIDDLE EAST/WEST)**—what was going on in other areas of the world? (This category is "Beyond the Middle East" during the biblical eras. As the focus of Christian history shifts toward Europe, after A.D. 100, this category changes to "Beyond the West.")

The categories in most eras have more information to display than will fit in the small Other Happenings window, so use the scroll bar to move the text up and down.

⊕ *The Spotlight window to the right will give detailed information about certain prominent historical figures and events.*

Jan's History Paper

It was one of those semi-awkward moments for Jan. She had just gotten out of youth group and she was waiting in the church lobby for her dad to finish his Christian education meeting. Mr. Halloran was there, too, waiting for his wife, who was in the same meeting. There was nothing wrong with Mr. Halloran—he was a friend of the family. Jan knew him well enough to say hi, but what else? That was the problem. She couldn't ignore him, but he was 40 years older than she was. What could they possibly talk about? She hoped her dad's meeting would be done soon.

Apparently Mr. Halloran had the same problem. He tried to make some lame small talk. "So, Jan, how's school?"

"Okay, I guess. For school."

Silence.

"What classes are you taking?"

"Geometry, which I hate. And history, which I love."

"Oh, really?" Mr. Halloran brightened. "I'm something of a history buff myself. What period are you studying?"

"Right now it's the colonial period in America. Before the revolution."

The older man gazed up at a corner of the ceiling, as if remembering a personal conversation with Ben Franklin. "A great time. Have they taught you anything about the Great Awakening?"

"I don't think so." Jan looked clueless.

"It was a religious revival," Mr. Halloran explained. "Sometimes I think that if it weren't for the Great Awakening, the American Revolution might never have happened."

"Wow."

It sounded as if Mr. Halloran might start giving a history lecture right on the spot, so Jan was kind of glad when her dad popped out of the meeting room. As much as she liked history, she wasn't about to give it any attention at this hour. But when her history teacher assigned a term paper the next day, she remembered Mr. Halloran's comments.

"Dad," she asked at dinner, "where would I find out about the Great Awakening?"

"The what?"

"A revival in the 1700s," she sighed, as if everyone was supposed to know that. "The Great Awakening."

Mom piped up. "You could try that *iLumina* program we got. Honestly, there is stuff in there I never dreamed of."

So Jan booted up the program and started looking around. She had seen her younger brother watching some animated Bible stories on it, but she hadn't used it much and wasn't really sure what she would find. She intuitively scanned the menu—Time Travel? That was intriguing. And maybe even related to history. She clicked on its Welcome screen and moused over the pictures until she got to "The Age of Reason and Revival 1648–1789." Clicking there, she saw those centuries spread out across the screen. The Great Awakening was mentioned there along with Jonathan Edwards. Jan had never heard of him, so she read more about his life in the Spotlight panel. She followed the trail to learn about George Whitefield and John Wesley. Then she looked up all three men in the Encyclopedia section.

Later that night, her mom asked if *iLumina* had been of any help to her.

"This is going to be one of my very best papers," she responded. "I really think that if it weren't for the Great Awakening, the American Revolution might never have happened."

CHAPTER TWELVE

⊖ MEDIA CENTER
welcome screen

HERE'S THE VISUAL dazzle that makes *iLumina* unique. The Media Center Welcome screen is your entry point into state-of-the-art animations, Virtual Tours, and Points in Time, as well as hundreds of photos and maps.

MEDIA CENTER FEATURES
To access the Media Center features, click on the picture labeled with the name of the feature you'd like to look at.

ANIMATIONS
iLumina contains 25 animations that bring the Bible vividly to life. *iLumina Gold* contains 35. Each animation is carefully and professionally rendered by highly skilled animators to bring you cutting-edge digital images. *iLumina* utilizes QuickTime technology to allow you to view these animations in the highest quality possible on your computer screen.

BIBLE ATLAS
To understand biblical events, it helps to know the territory. *iLumina* has scores of Bible maps that help you do just that. Trace the pilgrimage of Abraham, the wilderness wanderings, or the ministry of Jesus. Zoom in or out, print or take a Snapshot.

GUIDED VIRTUAL TOURS
iLumina includes Guided Virtual Tours which allow you to have a guide show you around various sites in the Holy Land. Our guides appear on video clips and provide helpful historical and archaeological information as well as reflection on and insight into biblical truth.

PHOTOS
You can browse through hundreds of high-quality photos of biblical sites and ancient objects. Most of these can be printed

HOW DO I GET HERE?
On the menu bar, click on
MEDIA CENTER.

WHAT'S HERE?
Links to Media Center
features

**WHERE CAN I GO
FROM HERE?**
Any of the Media Center
features in your version of
iLumina

HISTORY:
Animations were actually the beginning of the *iLumina* project. Animator Nelson Saba shared with Tyndale House his dream of animating the whole Bible. Publishers and editors at Tyndale House shared their own dream of a highly creative and practical Bible software. The two dreams merged, and you're looking at the result.

⊕ *Choose a Media Center feature
and click away!*

NOTE

You'll see photos in the Bible screens, accompanying Encyclopedia articles, and dotting the Time Travel eras. All these photos are catalogued and available here in the Media Center.

out and shared with your family or Sunday school class. The versatile Snapshot feature lets you copy the image to your computer clipboard to paste into a graphics program.

POINTS IN TIME

Points in Time are a combination of *iLumina*'s animations and Virtual Tours. While viewing some of the animations, you can pause the action and virtually step into the scene and look around. You can see characters up close, get information about objects that appear in the scene, and sometimes even venture out into surrounding areas in the Virtual Tours.

VIRTUAL TOURS

Imagine walking through the streets of Jerusalem as it was in the time of Christ. You can enter the temple complex and admire the beautiful Holy Place—even venture into the Holy of holies and see the spot where the ark of the covenant once stood. Based on extensive archeological research, the Virtual Tours give you a first-hand glimpse into a long-ago world. By merely dragging on your computer screen, you'll have the sense of walking through Jerusalem, visiting the tabernacle, or rushing to the empty Garden Tomb.

Going for the Gold

The Standard Edition of *iLumina* has all the same types of media found in *iLumina Gold*, but Gold has more content in each category (except maps). More photos, more animations, more Points in Time.

The Virtual Tours have been a major area of development for *iLumina*'s artisans. The Gold edition has several special features, such as audio tour guides, characters you can interact with inside the scenes, and various items to look at and learn about. There's also a Guided Tour of Jerusalem as it is today, with the capability of toggling between 2,000 years with a single click.

⊙ MEDIA CENTER
animations screen

DIGITAL ANIMATIONS of well-known Bible stories were one of the original features of *iLumina* when it was first dreamed up, and they've come a long way since. This screen is Animations Central—the place from which you can load up any animation included in *iLumina*. Watch as the familiar Bible stories come alive for you in a whole new way.

ANIMATIONS INDEX

On the left side of the screen, the Animations Index shows what animations are available to you. Click on the title of any animation to view it in the Animation Viewer.

ANIMATION VIEWER

The Animation Viewer is where the Bible stories come alive before your eyes in digital animation. After you click on any title in the Animations Index, that animation will begin playing automatically. At any time you can click the **PAUSE** button on the Animations toolbar or click right on the Animation Viewer itself to pause the play of the animation. Click again to resume playing. Or click the **STOP** button to reset the animation to the beginning.

TITLE, CAPTION, AND COPYRIGHT AREAS

Each animation has a title (which you see in the Index), and since the animations in *iLumina* are narrated directly from Scripture, you'll see the appropriate text verse by verse in the caption area just below the Animations toolbar. In the upper-right corner of the Animation Viewer (to the right of the title) is the reference of that Bible text. Click on that to go to the Bible section and check out the context of the story.

HOW DO I GET HERE?
- On the menu bar, click on MEDIA CENTER and then click Animations in the drop-down menu.
- Click on the Animations picture in the Media Center Welcome screen (see page 133).
- Click the MEDIA CENTER button when viewing an animation in the Media window in the Bible or Encyclopedia (see pages 94, 122).

WHAT'S HERE?
- Animations Index
- Animation Viewer
- Title, copyright, and caption area
- Animations toolbar
- Media Links bar

WHERE CAN I GO FROM HERE?
- Any animation included in your version of *iLumina*.
- Link to the Bible passage covered by the current animation.
- Jump to related Bible verses, Encyclopedia articles, and other areas of *iLumina* using the Media Link bar.

ANIMATIONS TOOLBAR

The Animations toolbar appears immediately under the Animation Viewer.

The **PLAY/PAUSE** button does double duty. When the animation is playing, it's a Pause button. When paused, it's a Play button.

Click **STOP** at any time to halt the animation and automatically rewind it to the beginning.

To the right of these buttons you'll see a **PROGRESS SLIDER**. The little round handle moves along the horizontal bar as the animation plays, giving you an idea of how much time remains. You can drag the handle along the bar to start playing the animation from any point you wish.

The **VOLUME** button brings up a dialog box where you can adjust the volume.

The **SNAPSHOT** button (with a picture of a camera) is one of the most exciting features on the page. You can use this button to take a freeze-frame shot of the animation at any point during play. The animation does not need to be paused for you to take a snapshot, although you can do that if you like. Whenever you click the Snapshot button, the frame on the screen will be copied to your computer's clipboard. You can also choose to save the image to a file for later use in a graphics program or to your Snapshots folder for later use in My Study Center (see page 72).

For maximum impact, try viewing the animation in Theater Mode by clicking the **THEATER MODE** button next to the Snapshot button. Theater Mode allows you to view the animation in nearly full-screen format. This is ideal for presentations on overhead screens in Sunday school classes, classrooms, churches, etc. (see page 59).

Some animations are linked to a Point in Time (see page 55). When a Point in Time is available for the current animation, the **POINT IN TIME** button (at the right end of the toolbar) will begin flashing. Click the **POINT IN TIME** button to jump into the Point in Time for this animation. You can jump back to the Animations Page by clicking the **BACK** button.

MEDIA LINKS BAR

The Media Links bar is located at the lower-right corner of the screen. This vertical bar is dynamic, meaning that the buttons that are visible will change depending on what links are available for the current animation. *iLumina* is based on interlinking content, and the animations in the Media Center are no exception. Every animation has a Bible link, and many have an Encyclopedia link, Time Travel link, or other links. Click on any link button to jump to the related content for the current animation.

The basic sectional buttons look like this:

Look for the color-coding on these sectional buttons:

- **BLUE:** Bible

- **RED:** Encyclopedia

- **GOLD:** Time Travel

Then special icons denote links to other media:

 Animation

 Map

Point in Time

The house next to the amphitheater in Virtual Jerusalem is our 21st-century office (see page 58). Wander down the hall and turn right until you enter a big blue room with tall cameras and an odd-looking person. (Well, odder than usual.) This is the motion capture room (in the biz, it's "mocap"). The artists put an actor in this suit to generate a computer image of a character's movements. And it's a riot at costume parties. Click on the suit to see the results of this mocap.

© When the Point in Time button flashes, as in the animation of Jesus healing the blind man, you can click on it to go to a Point in Time.

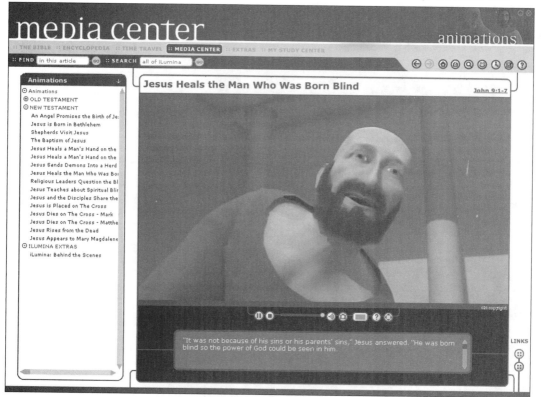

media center · animations

:: THE BIBLE :: ENCYCLOPEDIA :: TIME TRAVEL :: **MEDIA CENTER** :: EXTRAS :: MY STUDY CENTER

:: FIND in this article [GO] :: SEARCH all of iLumina [GO]

Animations

⊙ Animations
⊕ OLD TESTAMENT
⊙ NEW TESTAMENT
An Angel Promises the Birth of Jes
Jesus is Born in Bethlehem
Shepherds Visit Jesus
The Baptism of Jesus
Jesus Heals a Man's Hand on the
Jesus Heals a Man's Hand on the
Jesus Sends Demons Into a Herd
Jesus Heals the Man Who Was Bor
Religious Leaders Question the Bli
Jesus Teaches about Spiritual Blir
Jesus and the Disciples Share the
Jesus is Placed on The Cross
Jesus Dies on The Cross - Mark
Jesus Dies on The Cross - Matthe
Jesus Rises from the Dead
Jesus Appears to Mary Magdalene
⊙ ILUMINA EXTRAS
iLumina: Behind the Scenes

Jesus Heals the Man Who Was Born Blind   John 9:1-7

"It was not because of his sins or his parents' sins," Jesus answered. "He was born blind so the power of God could be seen in him.

LINKS

⊛ MEDIA CENTER
virtual tours screen

IMAGINE WALKING THROUGH Jerusalem in the time of Christ. What if you could actually stand at the foot of the cross or step into the empty tomb? *iLumina* gives you the opportunity to visualize those experiences. This screen is your first step in an adventure that will keep you busy for days (nights, too, if you're not careful). Just be sure you don't get lost.

VIRTUAL TOURS INDEX

On the left side of the screen, the Virtual Tours Index shows you what's available. Click on any entry and that scene will unfold in the Virtual Tour Viewer.

Titles in the Index are grouped into several different tours. For example, the first category listed in the index is Jerusalem. Click on **JERUSALEM** to expand the list and see all the places in Jerusalem where you can start your tour.

VIRTUAL TOUR VIEWER

The Virtual Tour Viewer, in the center of the screen, is where you will actually interact with the Virtual Reality technology. *iLumina*'s Virtual Tours are based on the latest digital imagery to bring you the most realistic experience possible. As you make your way through the streets of first-century Jerusalem, pay attention to the detail all around you. You'll be amazed at the lifelike textures, as well as the 360-degree world you can explore!

You "move" through this world by clicking your mouse on the picture itself and holding down the mouse button as you drag your mouse back and forth. As you move the mouse, the picture moves with you, so you feel as if you're turning around. You can turn in a complete circle and look up at the sky or down at the ground.

HOW DO I GET HERE?
* On the menu bar, click MEDIA CENTER and then click VIRTUAL TOURS in the drop-down menu.
* Click the "Virtual Tours" picture on the Media Center Welcome screen (see page 133).
* Click the MEDIA CENTER button when viewing a virtual tour in the Media window of the Bible or the Encyclopedia.

WHAT'S HERE?
* Virtual Tours Index
* Virtual Tour Viewer
* Map Thumbnail
* Virtual Toolbar
* Title and caption area
* Media Links bar

WHERE CAN I GO FROM HERE?
* You can go into first-century Jerusalem, or the Israelite tabernacle via Virtual Tour.
* Or link to Points in Time by clicking the POINT IN TIME button where it appears in the virtual tours (see page 56).
* Use the Media Links bar to link to the Bible, Encyclopedia, and other areas of *iLumina* that contain content related to your tour.

TIP

Anywhere in the Media Center, you can click on the title bar of the Index on the left to access another type of media.

You can "walk" from place to place by clicking on the path in front of you—as long as it's clickable. You'll know when it's clickable because glassy blue spheres will hover at eye level along the path. Click then to jump to the next location.

It's as if you are inside a bubble. Certain areas on the wall of this bubble are clickable. (The programmers call these areas "hotspots.") When you click, you move to another bubble.

The *iLumina* Virtual Tours are set up so that you will never jump to a location that is not visible from the previous location. In other words, when you click a hotspot leading down a street, you'll find yourself just a few yards down the street from the location you just left. If you click a hotspot leading into a building, you'll go first to the doorway, then click again to move all the way inside. If you want to go back, just "turn around" by dragging the picture 180 degrees and click back the way you came. (You can also use the Virtual toolbar buttons to go back.)

Be warned: you can spend hours wandering through the streets of Jerusalem, exploring the temple and tabernacle, following Jesus' steps down the Via Dolorosa, and more. Don't start exploring right before bedtime or when you need to study or eat!

NOTE

If you want a tutorial, don't miss the "Virtual Tour Tutorial" on pages 46–52.

THUMBNAIL MAP

At the lower left of the screen is a small map that helps you get your bearings as you explore. The Thumbnail Map rotates right along with the picture in the Virtual Tour Viewer so you always know what direction you are looking. The Map also has routes on it with all the tour stops (nodes) visible, so you'll know where you can go and where you can't. You can also drag the field of vision shown on the map around if you wish to see things from a different angle.

VIRTUAL TOOLBAR

The Virtual toolbar opens up even more options for you to get the most out of your virtual adventure. The toolbar is located just below and to the left of the Virtual Tour Viewer, and just to the right of the Thumbnail Map. From left to right, starting with the top row, the buttons are:

THUMBNAIL SWITCHER: this diagonal double arrow allows you to shift the Thumbnail Map from the corner to the main screen, switching places with the scene from the tour.

 ZOOM OUT: the minus magnifying glass zooms out, giving the impression of stepping backwards in the scene, getting a longer view.

⊕ **ZOOM IN:** the plus magnifying glass zooms in, giving the impression of stepping forward.

On the bottom row are the familiar buttons:

·)) **VOLUME CONTROL:** a dialog box will let you set the volume anywhere from "0" to "10" for the tour guide's voice and occasional music.

◉ **SNAPSHOT:** You can "snap a picture" of any Virtual Tour scene, saving it for My Study Center or another application.

SECRET

If you've stumbled into our office (via the house next to the amphitheater in Virtual Jerusalem—see page 58), just left of the entrance is the main work room, where most of the artist-technicians have been slaving away to create *iLumina*. Start clicking on their computer screens. One of them will take you to the finished product of whatever they're working on.

⊕ *Clicking the Volume button will bring up the Volume dialog box.*

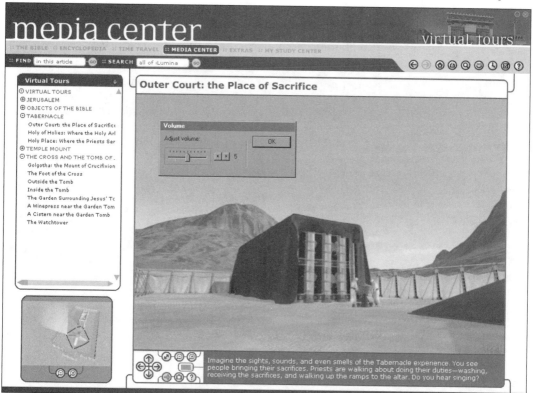

SIZE SELECTOR: As with the animations, you can do the Virtual Tours in Theater Mode, nearly filling your computer screen.

 HELP BUTTON: You mean this book isn't giving you all the help you need? Well!

TITLE AND CAPTION AREAS

If you've entered the house next to the Jerusalem amphitheater in the Virtual Tours, you've already slid through time into the office where *iLumina* has been made (see page 58). Down the hall on your right, you'll find the "Avid room," a small, dark room with three screens and some state-of-the-art Avid animation equipment. Click on a screen to see the final result of that process.

Each location has a name, which appears in the Title area, just above the Virtual Tour Viewer. As you move from place to place, the title will update, so you'll always know where you are. And as you move your mouse pointer around the screen, certain areas of the screen will pop up a description into the caption area, just underneath the Viewer. This is helpful for identifying certain objects, getting specific information about various items, and following a tour guide.

MEDIA LINKS BAR

The Media Links bar in the lower right corner of the screen provides a number of links to other areas of *iLumina*. The buttons will appear and disappear depending on what links are available at any particular time (See page 136).

⊘ MEDIA CENTER
theater mode

WHY DO PEOPLE enjoy going to a movie theater when they could just as easily stay home and rent a video? Why do people spend money on large-screen TVs when they could buy one half the size for a quarter of the price? Simple: the bigger the picture, the better the experience! That's what Theater Mode is all about. Stretch your computer monitor's capacity to the limit with full-sized photos, animations, virtual tours, and more! View animations and photos in the theater standard 16:9 widescreen. Or project *iLumina* onto an overhead screen for a presentation. You can do it all in Theater Mode!

THEATER AREA
Whatever you were looking at when you launched into Theater Mode, that's what you see in full screen. You can change the content of the Theater area by using the arrow buttons in the Media toolbar (see below).

MEDIA TOOLBAR
The Media toolbar appears at the top center of the screen, above the Theater area. Some of the buttons available in the toolbar vary, depending on what kind of media you are looking at. The arrows right and left allow you to change the content that appears in the Theater area. If, for example, you're watching an animation and you click the right arrow button, it will close that animation and open the next one listed in the Animations Index. The **SNAPSHOT** button does the same thing in Theater Mode that it does everywhere else: You can take a picture of anything currently showing in the Theater area and save the image to a file on your computer for later use in a graphics program, save it to your Snapshots folder for later use in My Study Center (see page 72), or copy it to your computer's clipboard.

HOW DO I GET HERE?
You can get to Theater Mode from any Media Center screen or from the Media window in the Bible or Encyclopedia by clicking the SIZE SELECTOR button.

WHAT'S HERE?
● Theater area
● Media Toolbar
● Title and caption area

WHERE CAN I GO FROM HERE?
● Use the RETURN button to go back where you came from.
● The MEDIA CENTER button will take you back to the Media Center Welcome screen.

⊛ *Use Theater Mode for a full-screen display of any graphic in the Media Center.*

When you are watching an Animation in Theater Mode, in addition to those three buttons, you have the controls from the Animations toolbar: a **PLAY/PAUSE** button, a **STOP** button (which also resets to the beginning), a **PROGRESS SLIDER** (showing how far along in the animation you are), a **VOLUME** button, and a **POINT IN TIME** button, which will flash whenever you get to a point in an animation where a Point in Time is available.

When you are exploring a Virtual Tour or a Point in Time, you have the arrows right and left, the **SNAPSHOT** button, and also buttons to **ZOOM OUT, ZOOM IN**, and control **VOLUME**. Zooming, of course, moves you virtually closer to or farther away from the image. When you are viewing a Virtual Tour or Point in Time, navigate by dragging the image in the Theater area just as you would in the Virtual Tour screen of the Media Center.

Be aware that extreme close-ups or wide-angle zooms may skew the panning somewhat. To correct this, zoom back in or out until the view is roughly the same as it was when you started.

You can always get back to the Media Center by clicking the **MEDIA CENTER** button in the upper-right corner of the screen. If you entered Theater Mode from a Media window in the Bible or Encyclopedia (see pages 94 and 122), you can return there by clicking the **RETURN** button at the extreme upper-right.

TITLE AND CAPTION AREAS

As in the Media Center and Media window, Theater Mode contains a caption area and a title area to display the name of the media element you are viewing and the accompanying Scripture or descriptive text, along with any copyright information. Use the scroll bar to move the text up and down if necessary.

iLumina and Family Devotions

It's not that her kids were badly behaved. They were just going through a stage. A "behaving badly" stage. Sam and Janet were at their wits' end. When the kids hit those odd numbers—eleven, nine, and seven—it was as if they took a vote and decided to be holy terrors. No, *holy* is the wrong word there—there was no holiness involved.

Even before the kids came along, Sam and Janet began to have family devotions every night. So their children were brought up with this tradition, but it had become such a struggle lately that they had decided to try it just once a week. They wanted to make it special. If prayer and Bible reading became a drudgery for the kids, what good would that do? And frankly, Sam and Janet were just tired of fighting about it.

One day Janet was talking with her friend Maria, who had kids about the same age as Janet's. Maria was talking about this new Bible software called *iLumina*. "And the kids love it," she said. "I can't steer them away."

Janet had often felt that Maria's kids were some kind of aliens—aliens from the Extremely-Well-Behaved Planet. Which is not to say that Janet was *jealous* of Maria—no, she was *very* jealous of Maria. Janet had read the same books, gone to the same seminars, and listened to the same Christian radio programs as Maria. So why were Maria's kids like the Brady Bunch while Janet's were like the Osbournes? What did Maria have that Janet didn't?

Well, she had *iLumina* for one thing.

Janet knew that no computer program could make her children good, but maybe it could entertain them enough to get some biblical teaching into them. She drove out to Target and got a copy. She became rather proficient with the program while the kids were at school. And that night at dinner she made an announcement. "Children, we're going to try not doing family devotions for a while. It's obvious that you all hate it, and your father and I are tired of forcing you. Right, dear?"

Sam gave Janet a look that said, *What on earth are you doing?*

Janet returned a look that said, *Trust me, honey. I've got a plan.*

"Right, dear," Sam answered, tentatively.

The kids were dumbfounded.

"Besides," Janet continued, "I got a new computer program today that I want to share with your father, and it's probably beyond your level. I wouldn't want you kids to be bored."

And so it began. After dinner every night, Sam and Janet went to the computer in the recreation room and read the Bible together on *iLumina*. Sometimes they looked things up in the Encyclopedia or the Time Travel section. Sometimes they pulled up the charts or Bible studies. And fairly often, they watched the animations.

By the third night, Rebekah, their youngest, came up beside them and wanted to see what they were doing. "Don't you have TV to watch?" Janet asked.

"This looks better," said the seven-year-old as she snuggled up to them.

By the end of the week, Josh, the middle kid, was begging to play with the Virtual Tours. A week later, Michael, the oldest, joined in.

Oh, they were still rambunctious. The kids regularly tested their parents' patience. But for a half-hour after dinner each night, this family had fun around God's Word. And that's a good thing on any planet.

⊕ MEDIA CENTER
points in time screen

A POINT IN TIME allows you to pause an animation and virtually step right into the story and look around. You can turn 360 degrees for a complete virtual interaction, clicking on various items (or characters) for an in-depth description. And you can sometimes take a virtual tour of that biblical setting.

POINTS IN TIME INDEX

Along the left side of the screen, the Points in Time Index lists the titles of all the Points in Time available in your version of *iLumina*, grouped by the animation they are linked to. Some animations contain several Points in Time; others have only one or none at all. Click on any title to load that Point in Time into the Points in Time Viewer.

POINTS IN TIME VIEWER

The action takes place in the Points in Time Viewer, the large area in the middle of the screen. When you click a title in the Points in Time Index, that Point in Time begins here. You can interact with the Point in Time in the same way you'd navigate through a Virtual Tour (see page 139). Drag your mouse anywhere on the image. The "eye" of the virtual camera will swivel in the same direction as your mouse, enabling you to "look around" the scene.

In some Points in Time, you will see a button with a diamond appear somewhere in the scene. This button is a link to a Virtual Tour. Click it to leave the Point in Time and jump into a Virtual Tour in the exact same location. For example, when you're viewing the Point in Time of the blind man washing in the Pool of Siloam, you can click the button that appears in the scene to leave the Point in Time and enter the

HOW DO I GET HERE?
- On the menu bar, click MEDIA CENTER and then click POINTS IN TIME in the drop-down menu.
- Click the POINTS IN TIME link on the Media Center Welcome screen (see page 133).
- Click the MEDIA CENTER button while viewing a Point in Time in the Bible or the Encyclopedia.
- Click the POINT IN TIME icon while watching an animation.

WHAT'S HERE?
- Points in Time Index
- Points in Time Viewer
- Thumbnail Map
- Points in Time toolbar
- Title and caption area
- Media Links bar

WHERE CAN I GO FROM HERE?
- Explore all of *iLumina*'s many Points in Time all in one place.
- Go to the animation the current Point in Time is linked to.
- In some Points in Time, step into the Virtual Tour of that setting.
- Link to the Bible, Encyclopedia, and other areas of *iLumina* via the Media Links bar.

Virtual Tour. You're still in the Pool of Siloam, but now you no longer see any characters, and you're free to move about the city of Jerusalem from there. (For more information on using Virtual Tours, see page 40.)

Some Points in Time are linked to *iLumina*'s Guided Tour feature. A video clip will appear with a guide to explain some interesting facts about the event or share an insight on how you can apply this Bible story to your life.

THUMBNAIL MAP

In the Virtual Tour, get to the big work room of our offices (see secrets on page 58 and page 141). See the United States flag? The *iLumina* creators actually come from different countries, and we know *iLumina* users do too. But we are privileged to work in this free land. Click on the flag to see some history of a foundational time in America's spiritual history.

The Thumbnail Map appears in the lower-left corner of the screen, allowing you to keep track of which direction you are facing. As you swivel around in the Points in Time Viewer, the Thumbnail Map will show you where your field of vision is.

POINTS IN TIME TOOLBAR

The Points in Time toolbar contains several tools that will help you make the most of your virtual experience. Click the **ZOOM** buttons to zoom in or out of the picture. (Be aware that at extremely high or low zooms, the swiveling might start to look strange. If this happens, just reverse the zoom to approximately the original level.) The **SNAPSHOT** button allows you to take an instant picture of whatever appears in the Points in Time Viewer at that moment. With this tool you can develop a virtually limitless library of still shots. You can opt to save your Snapshot to a file on your computer for later use in a graphics program, save it to your Snapshots folder for later use in My Study Center (see page 162), or copy it to your computer's clipboard. The **THEATER MODE** button lets you view the Point in Time in Theater Mode (see page 59). The **ANIMATION** button allows you to switch back and forth between the Point in Time and the animation to which it is linked.

Come to our office by entering the house next to the Jerusalem amphitheater (see page 58). Turn left and left again into the office of *iLumina* creator Nelson Saba. If you can tidy up the place, we'd appreciate it. But you could also click on the map on the wall and see where it takes you.

TITLE AND CAPTION AREAS

The title of the current Point in Time appears in the title area at the top of the Point in Time Viewer. To the right of the title is the Bible reference of the story you are looking at. Click the reference to jump right to that story in the Bible text. Below the Points in Time Viewer and to the right of the toolbar is the caption area. The Points in Time contain numerous comments on characters and objects within them. Mouse around the screen to see these comments pop up in the caption area.

MEDIA LINKS BAR

The Media Links bar in the lower right corner of the screen provides links to other areas of *iLumina*. The buttons will appear and disappear depending on what links are available at any particular time. (See page 136.)

If you're not sure where those Media Links buttons at the lower right will take you, hold your mouse over them for a few seconds. A tooltip will appear, describing each button.

⊕ *When you click the Snapshot button, a dialog box will appear and let you decide where to put the image.*

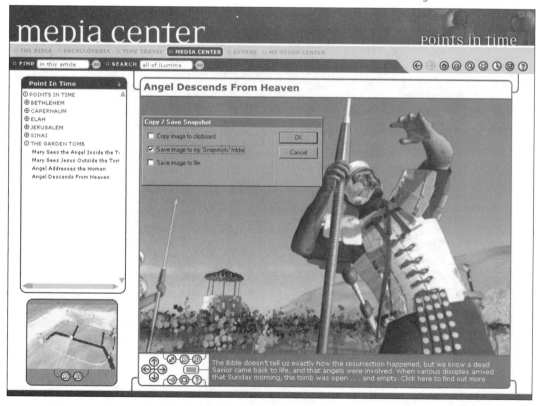

⊜ MEDIA CENTER
photos screen

iLumina comes packed with hundreds of photos to make your venture into the world of the Bible as visual as possible. One of the best ways to learn is by actually seeing the places and things you're learning about, and *iLumina* makes that possible by providing you with a central area to browse through all the photos you see elsewhere in the program, plus many more.

PHOTOS INDEX

In the Photos Index at the left side of your screen, all *iLumina* photos are listed by title and sorted alphabetically. Click on the title of any photo to load it into the Photo Viewer. (Use the scroll bar to move the list up and down.)

PHOTO VIEWER

When you click on a title in the Photos Index, that photo appears in the Photo Viewer in the center of the screen. You'll notice that the Photo Viewer is quite a bit larger than the photo viewing areas in the Media window of the Bible and Encyclopedia pages. For your maximum visual impact, you can make the photos even bigger by viewing them in Theater Mode.

PHOTOS TOOLBAR

The Photos toolbar appears just below the Photo Viewer. Click the **THEATER MODE** button to view the photo in a nearly full-screen format. (Note that some photos will lose detail in the larger size.) Click the **SNAPSHOT** button to take an instant picture of the photo you are looking at. You have the option of copying the picture to your computer's clipboard,

HOW DO I GET HERE?
- On the menu bar, click MEDIA CENTER and then click PHOTOS in the drop-down menu.
- Click the PHOTOS picture on the Media Center Welcome screen (see page 133).
- Click the MEDIA CENTER button while viewing a photo in a Bible or Encyclopedia Media window.

WHAT'S HERE?
- Photos Index
- Photo Viewer
- Photos toolbar
- Photo caption area
- Media Links bar

WHERE CAN I GO FROM HERE?
- Link to Bible references and Encyclopedia articles from photo captions.
- Link to Bible references, Encyclopedia articles, and other media areas by using the links in the Media Links area (see below).

⊕ *The Media Center Photos screen.*

saving the image in your Snapshots folder, or saving the image to a file on your computer. You can then open the photo in a graphics editing program to save it in a different format, insert it into a document, print it, etc. The Snapshot feature is available so that you can use *iLumina*'s photos in any way you choose, but please be sure you are not violating any copyright laws in your use of the photos. Check under the permissions information in the Help section for specific information on what photos and images are allowed to be used outside *iLumina*. Any images exported from *iLumina* must be credited properly wherever they are displayed, and any images exported may only be used for nonprofit, noncommercial uses.

TITLE, CAPTION, AND COPYRIGHT AREAS

Every photo carries a title above it and a caption below the Photos toolbar. Some captions are too long to fit in the caption area; scroll up or down as necessary. There is usually some copyright information on the lower right edge of the photo. If you ever adjust the photo with your own graphics program, be sure you don't remove this copyright notice.

MEDIA LINKS BAR

The Media Links bar in the lower right corner of the screen provides a number of links to other areas of *iLumina*. The buttons will appear and disappear depending on what links are available at any particular time.

➔ MEDIA CENTER
bible atlas

THE BIBLE ATLAS has been significantly upgraded from the original *iLumina*. It still gives you access to every map in *iLumina*, but now you can use the Map Thumbnail to explore each map in detail, search the map titles to find the map you're looking for, take snapshots of maps, and much more.

MAPS INDEX

In the Maps Index, along the left side of the screen, you will find a list of all the maps in *iLumina*, grouped in various categories. When you click the Title bar of the Index, you can choose from a submenu of alternate categories. Or, if you prefer, you can browse through a list of every map. As with any index, look for plus signs—that means that entry has some subentries within it. Click the plus sign or the entry to spill out the contents. Click on the title of any map to load it into the Map Viewer.

MAP VIEWER

When you click on a title in the Index, that map appears in the Map Viewer, center screen. But usually you can't see all of it at once. The *iLumina* maps are so detailed that they typically take up more space than the Viewer provides. Move the map image around by dragging it with your mouse. You can also navigate around the map using the Maps toolbar buttons or the Map Thumbnail. You can see the entire map by viewing it in Theater Mode.

Some maps have special links embedded right into the map itself. Click on these links to jump to Virtual Tours related to those areas. For example, in many maps of Israel, you can click on the city of Jerusalem to jump to a virtual tour of that city.

HOW DO I GET HERE?
- On the menu bar, click on MEDIA CENTER and then click BIBLE ATLAS in the drop-down menu.
- Click the BIBLE ATLAS link on the Media Center Welcome screen (see page 133).
- Click any map in the Media window of the Bible or Encyclopedia sections.

WHAT'S HERE?
- Maps Index
- Map Viewer
- Map Thumbnail
- Maps toolbar
- Title and caption areas
- Media Links bar

WHERE CAN I GO FROM HERE?
- Link to the Bible reference associated with every map.
- Use the Media Links bar to jump to other areas of *iLumina* with related content.

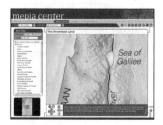

⊕ *The Bible Atlas contains over 350 maps.*

MAP THUMBNAIL

The Map Thumbnail is located below and to the left of the Map Viewer, just below the Maps Index. Whenever a map is visible in the Map Viewer, a smaller version of the complete map appears in the Map Thumbnail area. A red square indicates the area of the complete map that is currently visible in the Map Viewer. Drag that red square around the Thumbnail to change the contents of the Map Viewer accordingly. Or just click anywhere on the Map Thumbnail to make the red square jump to the spot you clicked. The viewable area in the Map Viewer will always change to match the area indicated by the red square in the Thumbnail.

MAPS TOOLBAR

Just to the right of the Map Thumbnail and below the Map Viewer, you'll find the Maps toolbar. At the top left of the toolbar are the **ZOOM** buttons. These will make the map in the Map Viewer larger or smaller, as you desire. Beneath the zoom buttons are four directional arrows. Use these buttons to move the viewable area of the map up or down, right or left. At the top right of the toolbar is the **SNAPSHOT** button, which will take a picture of the current map, which you can save to a file on your computer for later use in a graphics program, save to your Snapshots folder for later use in My Study Center (see page 72), or copy to your computer's clipboard. Below the Snapshot button is the **THEATER MODE** button. Click this button to view the entire map in Theater Mode.

TITLE AND CAPTION AREAS

Every map has a caption, which appears just below the Map Viewer and to the right of the Maps toolbar. The title of the map appears above the map, the same title that appears in the Maps Index. At the top right of the Map Viewer is a reference area that contains a link to a Bible passage associated with this map. Some captions also contain links to Bible verses. As with any Bible reference link, click on them to look them up.

MEDIA LINKS BAR

The Media Links bar is at the lower right corner of the screen. This bar is your reference point for links to other areas of *iLumina* that contain content related to the map you're looking at. The buttons visible in the toolbar will change depending on what links are available for the current map.

So you want to be a star? Make your way to our recording studio. (Jerusalem-theater-house-left-straight. Consult other secrets if necessary to figure out what that means.) If you see some computers and a keyboard, you're in the right place. Beyond the glass is the booth where the animations were recorded. The keyboard is where new music was created. Click on the keyboard to get a sample.

Pssst! Meet you in Nelson's office. (See secrets on page 58 and page 148 to get there.) Nelson's always been passionate about worship, especially the history of Jewish worship. So find the picture of the tabernacle on the wall and click on it. See what it became.

CHAPTER THIRTEEN

⊕ EXTRAS

welcome screen

THE MAKERS of *iLumina* have always envisioned this software as more than just another product. For many, it could become a whole new way of interacting with God's Word. In fact, those who use *iLumina*, and are enthused by it, could become a virtual community, sharing thoughts and ideas, feedback on new products, and the need for newer applications. Already some ministries have talked with Tyndale House about partnering on the production end, using the powerhouse of *iLumina* to enhance their worthy work.

Tyndale House is already planning on a special edition of *iLumina* for pastors, leaders, and teachers. That version will use the capabilities of *iLumina* to enhance the study of the Greek text of the New Testament, find the perfect quote or illustrations, and make visual presentations quickly and easily. As of this writing, those visions are well on their way to being a reality. Stay tuned to www.iLumina.com for upgrades, enhancements, and new products within the *iLumina* software line.

In the Extras screen you'll find a list of current *iLumina* products, links to new products and a link to the *iLumina* Web site. You can also contact our tech support staff from here.

EXTRAS INDEX

Additional information is grouped into two categories:

• The World of *iLumina* (news of *iLumina* products)

• Tech support (if you can't find answers in this book or from Help)

As always, click on any plus sign to see listings under that particular topic. Click on any entry to go to that feature.

HOW DO I GET HERE?
• **Click on EXTRAS on the** *iLumina* **home page.**
• **Click on EXTRAS in the menu bar.**

WHAT'S HERE?
• **Extras Index**
• **Welcome text area**
• **Web Links**

WHERE CAN I GO FROM HERE?
• **To the Internet to get tech support, customer service, or news of new products**
• **To a screen of Frequently Asked Questions (and their answers)**
• **To learn more about** *iLumina***'s photo partner**

⊕ *The Extras screen provides links to iLumina Technical Support.*

WELCOME TEXT AREA

When you first come to this screen, words of welcome appear in the center of the screen. If you click on a text-based feature (rather than a Web-based feature) in the Index, that text will appear here.

WEB LINKS

At bottom right, there are buttons you can click to connect with *iLumina*'s Web site. (This goes to the same site as several of the Index entries, it's just a shortcut for you.) **WHAT'S NEW** will take you to see new *iLumina* products, and **CHECK FOR UPGRADES** will help you find any available upgrades for *iLumina* products you already own.

Note that you need an Internet connection to do this. If you have that available, *iLumina* will automatically find it and use it. If you have an always-on connection or an automatic startup, *iLumina* should send you right to the Web. If not, it will bring up your sign-on screen, and you'll have to sign on before *iLumina* takes you to its site.

CHAPTER FOURTEEN

⊙ MY STUDY CENTER*
welcome screen

MY STUDY CENTER is a new feature introduced in *iLumina Gold*. Here you can search all of *iLumina* for raw material, then select some of it to edit in your own document. It's a workspace where you can efficiently interact with *iLumina*'s treasures.

Visualize My Study Center as a desktop with three panels—labeled **SEARCH**, **DISPLAY**, and **MY STUDY**. In the **SEARCH** panel, you can list the results of an Advanced search for words or phrases in any part of *iLumina*. The **DISPLAY** panel shows you the context of any search result you click on—an entire chapter or article. Then you can copy and paste pieces of the displayed material over to the **MY STUDY** panel, which functions as a word processor. You can write new material or edit what you have pasted there.

Now this is very important. In order to make this as usable as possible, *iLumina* could only fit two panels on the screen at a time. So you are always looking at *either* the search and Display panels or the Display and My Study panels. You can easily slide back and forth between the two views *without losing any material*. All three panels are always there, but you can only view two at a time. (You are invited to make your own spiritual application of that point.)

DESCRIPTION OF MY STUDY CENTER
The Welcome screen for My Study Center functions as an entrance screen but also gives you a concise overview of the three basic steps to using My Study Center: Advanced Search Results, Display, and the My Study. Simply click **START NOW** in the lower right to enter My Study Center.

HOW DO I GET HERE?
Click on MY STUDY CENTER in the menu bar, or on the *iLumina* home page.

WHAT'S HERE?
Description of My Study Center

WHERE CAN I GO FROM HERE?
Use the START NOW link to go to My Study Center.

⊕ *My Study Center's Welcome screen.*

Tim's Personal Devotions

Tim wanted to make this Easter special. Year after year he had sped through the season with hardly a nod to it. A new suit maybe. Dinner with his folks. A Good Friday service here and there. But this year he wanted to really observe the season, in all its sacred specialness.

He wasn't sure how he would do this . . . until he started experimenting with the *iLumina* program he had received for Christmas. He was especially interested in the animations, along with the Points in Time and the Virtual Tours. With these tools, he figured, he could practically relive the events of Passion Week.

As the week approached, he blocked out an hour per day in his schedule, from Palm Sunday to Easter Sunday. That time would be devoted to prayer, reflection, and study, with reading enhanced by the visual elements of *iLumina*.

For Palm Sunday, he read the accounts of the Triumphal Entry from all four Gospels. It's not absolutely certain where Jesus would have entered the city, but Tim imagined the procession arriving from the south, near the Pool of Siloam, and ascending the terraced streets to the Temple Mount. He followed this path on the Virtual Tour of Jerusalem. He saved the story of the moneychangers in the Temple for his Monday meditation. That's when he explored the Virtual Tour of the Temple Mount, visualizing where the sellers might have been, on the steps alongside the Temple itself.

On Tuesday and Wednesday, he read biblical stories that might have occurred on those days in the week before Jesus' crucifixion. He also consulted the commentaries available in *iLumina*. Thursday he watched the animation of the Last Supper, but then he clicked the Point in Time button to enter the scene and learn more about this Passover meal. Mousing over various dishes and cups, he read the captions that explained them.

Friday he read about the Crucifixion, and he followed the Virtual Tour from just outside the Temple Complex, by the Antonia Fortress, where Jesus probably faced trial. Then he followed along the streets of Jerusalem, went north through the

Damascus Gate, and over to Golgotha. Then he played the animation of the Crucifixion of Jesus.

For Saturday's meditation, he stayed in the Bible section, looking up some of the Old Testament prophecies about the Messiah, especially Psalm 22. Then Sunday morning, he jumped out of bed to play the Resurrection animation, clicking the Point in Time button to enter the tomb, and then exploring the Garden Tomb area. He finished his special week by reading Psalm 16 out loud in praise to his risen Lord.

Tim had never felt so close to the events surrounding Jesus' death and resurrection. What a blessing! Thinking back on his week, Tim decided to use My Study Center and make a document to commemorate his study and reflection. He took some snapshots of moments in the animations that really stood out in his memory. He cut and pasted some verses from the Gospels. Then he loaded these in the My Study Center Display window and pasted them into the My Study window. In the My Study window he was able to arrange them in a meaningful order and even keep a record of his own reflections on those Scriptures and images.

Could Tim have done something like this without *iLumina*? Sure. But the creative offerings of this new program helped him craft a memorable observance of this most holy time.

⊙ MY STUDY CENTER*
search screen

WITH MY STUDY CENTER, you can create your own document from material you find throughout *iLumina*, save it to a file on your computer, and then print it out for a project or report, or use it as a study help. It all starts here, with your *iLumina* search.

STUDY BAR

Sounds like a place college kids hang out, huh? Here it's the place you'll go to navigate through My Study Center. Elsewhere in *iLumina*, the bar under the menu bar is called the search bar. Here it's replaced with the Study bar, because there are several new options.

ADVANCED SEARCH DIALOG BOX

Clicking here will open a dialog box for an Advanced search of *iLumina*. Elsewhere in *iLumina*, you can do simple searches for a particular word. The Advanced search allows you a much greater degree of precision.

WITH ALL THESE WORDS. Type any words, in any order, into this box. My Study Center will search *iLumina* for any search unit that contains *all* the words you typed.

WITH THIS EXACT PHRASE. Type into this box a phrase you want to search for. Be sure to type the phrase exactly, because My Study Center will search *iLumina* for the exact text you entered.

WITH ANY OF THESE WORDS. Type any words, in any order, into this box. My Study Center will search *iLumina* for any search unit that contains *any one* or more of the words you typed.

WITHOUT THESE WORDS. Type any words you want to *exclude* from your search into this box. My Study Center will search *iLumina* for any search unit that contains the words or phrases you entered into the other boxes *and does not contain* any of the words you typed into this box.

HOW DO I GET HERE?
* On the menu bar, click MY STUDY CENTER, and then click MY STUDY on the drop-down menu.
* Click START NOW on the My Study Center Welcome screen.

WHAT'S HERE?
* Study bar
* Search Results panel
* Display panel

WHERE CAN I GO FROM HERE?
Click the large right arrow to enter the My Study screen.

MATCH CASE. Check this box if you want My Study Center to match the uppercase or lowercase letters of the words or phrases you entered. In most cases you can leave this box unchecked, because the capital letters aren't important. But if, for example, you type "God" into the search box and *don't* check the "Match Case" box, My Study Center will search for "god" as well as "God."

GO. Click this button when you're ready to begin your search. Most searches are very fast, but some complicated searches may take a while.

CANCEL. Click this button to close the dialog box without executing your search.

HELP. To get more assistance.

SIMPLE. Click this button to return the dialog box to the simple search dialog. From here you can search or return to the Advanced dialog box by clicking **ADVANCED.**

SEARCH LOCATIONS. My Study Center searches all areas of *iLumina* by default, but if you want, you can limit the search to certain areas of *iLumina*. Check the **CHECK/ UNCHECK ALL** box to check or uncheck all the locations at once. Then selectively add or remove checkmarks from areas you want to search or leave out.

After you start your search (by clicking **GO**), the search results will appear in the search panel on the left half of your screen.

LOAD SNAPHOTS

Click here to produce a list of the Snapshots you have taken in *iLumina*. This is an extremely helpful way to use *iLumina*'s media images in your own documents. Be warned, however, that this will appear in the Search Results panel, so save your search results first if you want to use them later.

SEARCH RESULTS

This button will produce a drop-down menu with three options for managing different lists from your searches. Click **SAVE AS** to save your search results for later use. They will be saved as a List file with the extension *.lst*. Once you have created some List files, you may either want to load a list from a previous search into the Search Results panel, or delete certain lists which are no longer of use to you. Those two functions are what the **LOAD** and **DELETE** commands are there for.

Notice that all three commands will open a dialog box showing the directory where your List files are stored. When you load a List file, its name will appear just to the right of the **MY STUDY** button in the Study bar.

MY STUDY

The drop-down menu from this button allows you to start a **NEW** study (clearing off the My Study panel), **SAVE** your current study, **LOAD** a study you've saved, **DELETE** a study, or **EXPORT** your study as discussed on page 80.

Files from My Study, like Search Results above, are saved as List files with the *.lst* extension. When you **LOAD** a study, its name will appear just to the right of the **MY STUDY** button in the Study bar. When you choose to **DELETE** a study, a dialog box will appear prompting you to select which file you wish to delete.

SEARCH RESULTS PANEL

The Search Results panel is in the left half of the screen, where your search results will be listed when you execute an Advanced search.

⊕ *The Load Snapshots button will put all your snapshots in the Search Results panel so you can view them in the Display panel.*

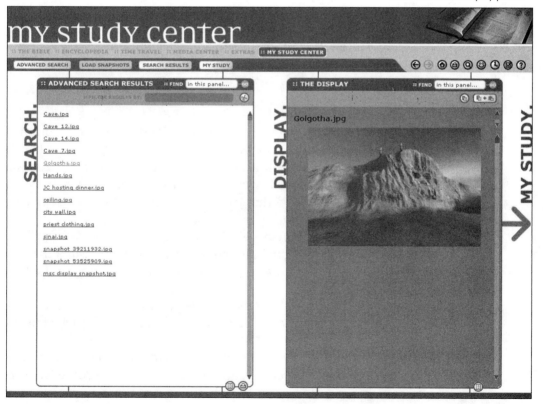

The search results are divided by *search unit*. If you searched the Bible, the results are listed by Bible *verse*. If you searched the Encyclopedia, *articles* are listed. In the Media Center, each photo, map, or animation is a search unit.

Each search result contains two parts: a title and an excerpt. For Bible searches, the title is the reference (Genesis 3:2 for example). For Encyclopedia listings, the title is the name of the article. The excerpt appears just under each title, either the whole Bible verse, or a line of Encyclopedia text containing the target word. The text you searched for will appear in bold within the excerpt.

When you click on any search-result title, the text of the search unit will appear in the Display panel.

At the top of the Search Results panel is a **FIND** box. Use this to narrow your search results even further. Some searches will list only a few items, but others may return thousands. You can highlight your more relevant search results by typing an additional keyword into the **FIND** box and clicking the **GO** button. Any search result that contains the text you searched for in its excerpt or title will now show that word in bold.

Perhaps you want to look at only Encyclopedia articles, or only verses from the NLT, or only Media images. You can filter your results by type (or search location) by clicking on the **FILTER RESULTS BY** menu and selecting a more specific category to look at.

DISPLAY PANEL

On the right half of the screen, the Display panel fills up with the full context of any entry you clicked on the search panel. If you clicked on a Bible verse, the whole chapter appears here, with your key verse at the top. If you selected an Encyclopedia article, the whole article appears here. You can also view media images in this space.

The Display panel functions like most other text areas in *iLumina*; you can highlight and copy text and search the text for words or phrases (use the Find box at the top of the Display panel).

When you've decided what you want to work with, highlight it in the text. Then you can click either the **COPY** button or the **COPY AND PASTE** button. The **COPY** button saves the material to your computer clipboard, awaiting a future Paste command. After copying the text, you can click the large arrow pointing right to slide the screen over to the My Study panel. Then position your cursor where you want the new text and click the **PASTE** command (or CTRL+V on your keyboard) to paste the text in place. Use **COPY AND PASTE** if you don't want to slide back and forth so much. When you highlight text and click the **COPY AND PASTE** button, it will automatically be pasted to the My Study screen even if you don't see the My Study screen. It will be pasted on your page wherever you last left your cursor.

If you have clicked in the search panel on the title of a Media element (such as a photo, map, or animation) then the Display panel becomes a Media window, just as you would see in the Bible section. You can use the same **COPY** and **COPY AND PASTE** buttons to move this material to the My Study panel, but it will go to the Media page on that panel.

What if you don't want to use what appears on the Display panel? Just click on another entry in the search panel and the new chapter, article, or whatever you click will appear there, replacing the old one.

If you don't highlight anything and just click COPY or COPY AND PASTE, the entire contents of the Display panel are copied or copied and pasted.

⊕ *The Display panel is to the right of the Search Results panel.*

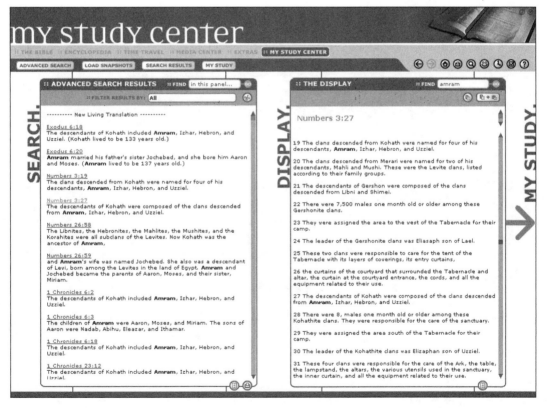

→ MY STUDY CENTER*
my study screen

THIS SCREEN IS where you can collect all your search results into one place, copy them onto a word processing page, and then edit, rearrange, rewrite, delete, save, and print the result. Whether you're preparing a sermon, writing a paper, or organizing your thoughts for personal study or devotions, the My Study screen is where you can make it happen.

DISPLAY PANEL

The Display panel on this screen is exactly the same as the Display panel you see on the My Study Center Search screen (see page 161). The **COPY** and **COPY AND PASTE** commands work the same way, except now you can see the My Study panel where you're pasting things. If the Display panel is blank, you'll have to slide over to the search screen (via the big arrow on the left) and start a new search or click on an existing search result in the search panel.

MY STUDY PANEL

On the right half of your screen, the My Study panel functions as a word processor on its text page. It starts out as a blank slate, but you can paste text here and add your own. Create your own document and then save it or print it.

Note that the My Study panel has two pages. You have a Text page and a Media page. Click on the tabs at the top to switch between those pages. Whenever you paste text from the Display panel, the Text page automatically comes to the foreground. Pasting a media image brings up the Media page. The Media page only displays one image at a time, but it can hold as many images as you like. Note that different buttons are available on the Media page than were on the Text page. A counter appears to the right to tell you whether you're

HOW DO I GET HERE?
From the Search screen in My Study Center, click on the large arrow on the right side of the screen to slide over to this screen

WHAT'S HERE?
• Display panel
• My Study panel

WHERE CAN I GO FROM HERE?
You can slide back to the search screen by clicking the large arrow on the left pointing left.

⊕ PAGE 167

viewing image "1 of 3" or "4 of 10." Click on the left and right arrows to move between images.

On its text page the My Study panel contains buttons with the following commands:

 CUT TEXT (CTRL+X) to Cut

 COPY TEXT (CTRL+C) to Copy

 PASTE TEXT (CTRL+V) to Paste material you have just cut or copied

 COPY AND PASTE moves an item from the display panel to the My Study panel

B **BOLD TEXT** (CTRL+B) to switch to Bold type

I **ITALICIZE TEXT** (CTRL+I) to switch to Italicized type

U **UNDERLINE TEXT** (CTRL+U) to switch to Underlined type

P **PLAIN TEXT** to switch back to Plain type

Simply highlight a portion of your text and click the appropriate command.

The My Study panel also has a **FIND** box, in case you've been working on the text for a while and can't remember where you saw or wrote something earlier. Just type in the word you're looking for and click **GO**—it will be highlighted wherever it appears in your text.

When you've used all the text from the Display panel that you need for the moment, you can go back and search some more. Click the big left arrow on the left side of the screen to slide back to the Search screen. Don't worry. Your My Study panel will be there when you come back, just as you left it. On the Search screen, you can fire up a new search, or just click on another search result, loading new text into the Display panel.

YOUR FINISHED WORK

When you're satisfied with the work you've done in the My Study panel, you can export the contents in two ways.

(1) You can save it to a file on your computer. Text is

saved in .rtf (Rich Text Format) files, which are readable in almost every word-processing program. Media images are saved in .jpg files. Click the **EXPORT** button, just above the word "Export," to the right of the My Study panel to do this. This will prompt you to choose a directory to save your work in. Your file will then be saved there with the sme name as the directory you chose to save it in.

(2) You can print the contents of the Text page and the Media Page. To do this, bring the page you want to print to the foreground of the My Study panel and click the **PRINT** button. A dialog box will come up, allowing you to give instructions to your printer.

SECRET

If you intend to crop media images or embed them within documents, the exported .html files might be difficult to work with. But any Snapshots you copy from the display window are available on your computer's clipboard; simply minimize *iLumina*, paste the photo into your favorite graphics editing program, and you're ready to go.

⊕ *From the Display panel you can cut and paste material into the My Study panel.*

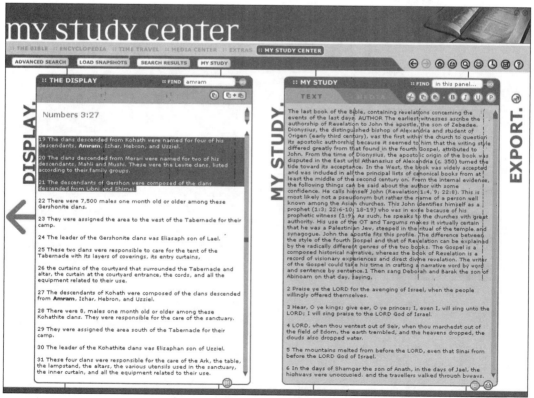

.LST (List files) File format used by *iLumina* to store search results and documents for My Study Center.

.PDF (Page Display Format) File format used by Adobe Reader for visual files, used in *iLumina* for Bible study guides and Bible charts.

.RTF (Rich Text Format) File format used for text documents and understood by virtually all word processing systems. When you export a text document from My Study Center to your computer, it is saved as an .rtf file.

ADOBE READER Text-reading program which uses .pdf files and is accessed automatically whenever you open a Bible study or Bible chart.

ADVANCED SEARCH Search function available in My Study Center, allowing a user to fine-tune a word search with various options. The Advanced Search helps you find what you want without listing entries you don't want.

ANIMATIONS Visual depictions of Bible stories (or objects) with sound and moving pictures.

ASTERISKS The symbol: *. Throughout this book, asterisks mark features that are only available in *iLumina Gold*, not in *iLumina* Standard. Within *iLumina,* in the text of the New Living Translation, asterisks mark verses that have text notes available. Click on the asterisk to see the note.

BIBLE ATLAS The collection of Bible maps included in the Media Center of *iLumina*.

BIBLE COMPANIONS Commentaries, notes, devotional aids, and other study helps available in *iLumina* to assist your understanding of the Bible text.

BIBLE OVERVIEW A screen in the Bible section of *iLumina* giving access to various survey information about the Bible, Bible books, and Bible versions.

BIBLE RESOURCE INDEX The right panel of the Bible Welcome screen, offering access to any book of the Bible, a thematic index of Bible verses, and other resources.

BIBLE STUDIES: *iLumina* offers Bible study guides on every book of the New Testament, with questions for discussion or personal reflection and some background information. These Bible studies can be printed out and used in small-group settings.

BLUEPRINT BROWSER A kind of table of contents for the Bible text that lists the section headings within Bible chapters.

CD-ROM Compact Disc-Read Only Memory. Most computers now have a CD drive in addition to a floppy disk drive.

CHARTS Helpful graphics on themes found throughout the entire Bible. These charts can be printed out and used in small-group settings.

CLIPBOARD A holding function of most computers, allowing you to copy material from one program and paste it into another program or in other places in a document.

COMMENTARY A resource that provides an explanation of the Bible text.

CONTEXT MENU A range of options available when you right-click on a Bible verse in *iLumina*. The menu appears on-screen, allowing you to summon a variety of resources associated with the verse you clicked.

CONTROL-CLICK On Macintosh computer systems, clicking the mouse while holding the CTRL key on the keyboard accomplishes the same as a right-click on other systems.

CONTROL BAR Our term for the adjustment controls in the Media window with various media elements. Each type of media has its own set of controls.

CROP To cut a media image (photo, map, or frame) to a particular shape or size. You cannot do this within *iLumina*, but you might find a way to copy a file to another graphics program and do so there.

CROSS-REFERENCES Bible verses that relate to the current verse you're reading.

CURSOR The visual cue (usually a flashing line or rectangle) that shows your location on a computer screen.

DEFAULT In any set of options, the default is what the computer chooses for you if you don't make any other choice.

DESKTOP *iLumina* also uses the term to denote the entire three-panel workspace in its My Study Center section.

DEUTERO-CANONICAL BOOKS Also known as the Apocrypha, books generally included between the Old Testament and New Testament in Roman Catholic Bibles, but not in those used by Protestants.

DEVOTIONAL Term referring to Scripture-related material that focuses on one's personal relationship with God, as opposed to more academic study of textual meaning or background.

DIALOG BOX A menu of options that appears, allowing you to set parameters for a search, for the printing of a document, or for other purposes.

DIRECTIONAL ARROWS (MAPS) Map controls that allow you to position a map within the screen just how you want it.

DISPLAY PANEL The center panel of the three panels in the My Study Center program. This displays the entire chapter, article, or other context of an entry listed on the Search panel. Material from this panel can be copied and pasted to the My Study panel.

DRAG (also referred to as "click and drag") A technique where you use the mouse click on a point on the screen and continue to hold the left mouse button down as you move the mouse. This is used to move through Virtual Tours, Points in Time, or Time Travel screens.

DROP-DOWN MENU Any list of options that appears when you click on or mouse over a particular spot.

DVD-ROM Digital Video Disc-Read Only Memory. Some newer computers use this system for data loading. A DVD holds much more information than a CD, so all of *iLumina*, which is contained on 4 CDs, fits on one DVD-ROM disc.

EXPORT To send text or images from the My Study panel to another place on your computer. You can save text in .rtf files or save images in .html files, or you can export the content to your printer.

FILTER RESULTS A way to sort through items in the Search panel of My Study Center, thus narrowing down your search.

FIND A space available in many of the index panels of *iLumina* and some text panels. Type in a word or phrase and *iLumina* will find it *within that current index or text*. This will not search all of *iLumina*. Use the search function for that.

FOCUS AREAS Categories of the Encyclopedia.

GREEN DIAMOND A flashing symbol that marks the portal between an animation or Virtual Tour and a Point in Time. Click on it to travel back and forth between these different media elements.

GUIDED VIRTUAL TOURS Audio (and sometimes visual) tour guides that assist on your Virtual Tours.

ICON Any symbol or picture on your computer screen that represents some program or function.

ILUMINA 2.0 AND GOLD *iLumina 2.0* is the more affordable version, with the bulk of *iLumina's* content, but it lacks My Study Center, the KJV, and some media images and Encyclopedia entries. *iLumina Gold* has all the features discussed in this book.

ILUMINA HOME PAGE The introductory display for all of *iLumina* or for any of its six major modules.

KJV (King James Version) The classic English Bible translation first published in 1611.

LIFE APPLICATION An emphasis on practical obedience to scriptural teachings. This emphasis is seen in many of the Bible Companions within *iLumina*.

LINKS Instant connections to other parts of *iLumina*. Click and you're there.

MAP THUMBNAIL A small representation of the area you're exploring in the center of the screen. Since many maps are larger than the main viewing area, the Bible Atlas uses the Map Thumbnail to show you what portion of the larger map is on screen. Thumbnail Maps also help you navigate through a Virtual Tour by offering a "You Are Here" placement.

MASTER TIMELINE The graphic at the top of any Time Travel Era screen that shows the placement of that era in the full sweep of human history.

MEDIA CHOOSER BAR In the Media Window that appears in the Bible text screen or the Encyclopedia screen, this bar at the top will allow you to select different media elements if there is more than one available.

MEDIA ELEMENT Any of the images included in *iLumina,* whether photos, maps, animations, Virtual Tours, or Points in Time.

MEDIA LINKS BAR A vertical strip of buttons at the lower right of most Media Center screens. The buttons are coded by color or icon to link you to related material in other sections of *iLumina.*

MEDIA TOOLBAR Any set of controls for media elements. Each type of element requires slightly different controls, but sometimes we refer to all of them as "media toolbars."

MEDIA WINDOW In the Bible text screen or Encyclopedia entry screen, the window where media elements appear.

MENU BAR The line across the top of *iLumina* screens, with the names of the major sections of the program: The Bible, Encyclopedia, Time Travel, Media Center, Extras, and My Study Center.

MY STUDY PANEL The right-most panel of the three panels in My Study Center. This functions as a word processor, allowing you to work with text and images you have pasted there—you can add new material as well.

MY STUDY SCREEN Sometimes we call this the Display/My Study screen. This is the view of My Study Center that shows the Display and My Study panels. You can move to the Search screen by clicking the large arrow pointing to the left.

MY STUDY TOOLBAR Controls available in the My Study panel that help you work with the text. You can Cut, Copy, or Paste and make basic adjustments to typeface.

NLT (New Living Translation) The newest translation of the Bible, first published in 1996.

OBJECT MOVIE A technical term for the rotating animations of Bible objects in *iLumina.* You probably don't need to know that, ex-

cept to know that the Virtual Tours of these objects don't have the same range of motion that the Bible scenes have.

OTHER HAPPENINGS WINDOW The window at the bottom of any Time Travel Era screen presenting the extra-biblical goings-on of that era. Categories include Culture, Technology, World Power, Religion, Philosophy, the Holy Land, and Beyond the Middle East (or West).

POINT IN TIME Think of it as a cross between an animation and a Virtual Tour. At certain points in an animated story, you can click the blue-diamond button and essentially freeze the story there. Then you can "enter" the scene, as you would in a Virtual Tour, using the same dragging technique to look around that scenario.

POINT IN TIME BUTTON The blue-diamond icon appears within certain animations and at certain places in Virtual Tours. Click on it to enter a Point in Time. The icon also appears on the Media Control bar; when this flashes, you can click on it to enter the Point in Time.

PRINTER DIALOG BOX A box that enables you to give precise commands to your printer. This appears whenever you click a print command in the toolbar or in My Study Center.

PROGRESS SLIDER A media control that works with animations only. The marker moves to the right along the bar as the animation plays. You can see how far along you are and drag the marker to start the animation at any point.

REFERENCE WINDOW A window in Bible text screens and many Encyclopedia screens which provides extra information on the main text. When reading the Bible, right-click in that window and choose which Bible Companion you want to use.

RIGHT-CLICK Your computer mouse probably has two buttons. The left one does most of the heavy lifting when you use your computer, but *iLumina* uses the click of the right button (on Bible text) to unleash a variety of options. (For Mac users, the equivalent is a mouse-click while holding down the CTRL button on your keyboard.)

SEARCH BAR The line under the menu bar that contains the Find and Search text boxes that allow you to search *iLumina* for particular words.

SEARCH RESULTS PANEL The left-most of the three panels in My Study Center. This panel lists the results of your searches. This is pretty raw data, just a verse or a line or two. Click on any entry in this Search panel to bring up the entire chapter or article (or media element, etc.) in the Display panel.

SEARCH SCREEN The screen containing the Search Results panel and the Display panel, sometimes called the Search/Display screen. This is where you do your initial search-and-gather work for a My Study Center project.

SIZE SELECTOR A media control that allows you to choose the size of the image display. We have small, large, and Theater Mode.

SNAPSHOT A function that records a copy of an image in a Snapshots folder within *iLumina*. If you're viewing an animation, the Snapshot will capture the frame showing when you click the camera icon on the Media Toolbar. You can view your Snapshots in My Study Center.

SPOTLIGHT A window on the right side of each Time Travel Era screen presents a timeline of a particular person who lived within that era. By clicking on the pictures along an era's timeline, you can find the Spotlights available in that era.

TEXT-SIZING BUTTONS In most screens where you view a document, you can make the letters larger or smaller by clicking the Text-sizing buttons. Click the large T to make the text larger, the small T to make it smaller. The page icon simply returns the text to its original size.

THEATER MODE A way of viewing media images that uses your entire computer screen.

THUMBNAIL MAP See *Map Thumbnail*.

THUMBNAIL SWITCHER A button with a diagonal arrow on the Control bar for the Virtual Tour, which allows you to swap the Thumbnail Map and the main picture in the Media Viewer so that the Thumbnail Map is magnified. This can help you get your bearings.

THUMBNAILS Thumbnails are small images of larger photos. When you see thumbnails in a Bible Photo window, click on any thumbnail to see a larger image of that photo.

TIME TRAVEL ERA One of 14 slices of human history in *iLumina's* Time Travel section. Each era has its own screen, with special Spotlights and Other Happenings info.

TITLE BAR A thin strip at the very top of a window or frame which gives a title (often a file name) to its contents. In *iLumina*, the title bars often contain drop-down menus which can change the window's contents.

TOOLTIPS Not sure what a particular button does? Just hold the cursor over it for a second or two. A description will appear in a little box next to the button. That description is a Tooltip. These also appear for index entries that are too wide for the window.

TOP TOPICS A focus area of the *iLumina* Encyclopedia featuring at least a hundred entries with additional media images and reference info.

VERSE FINDER A thematic index of the Bible accessible in the right panel of the Bible Welcome screen. Click on one of the available topics and choose from several pertinent verses.

VERSION SELECTOR In *iLumina Gold*, the Search bar has several spaces—Find, Search, the Bible reference space, and then a version selector. Click there and select the King James Version or the New Living Translation or see both side-by-side.

VIRTUAL TOURS One of five types of media available in the Media Center. Virtual Tours enable you to "enter" a biblical scene and explore it in 360 degrees. This gives the impression of being able to look around and walk through various sites in first-century Jerusalem.

ZOOM With maps, Virtual Tours, and Points in Time, click the icon of the magnifying-glass icon with a plus sign to make the image larger (zooming in). The magnifying-glass icon with a minus-sign makes it smaller (zooms out). You can also zoom in and out by using the SHIFT key (in) and the CTRL key (out) on your keyboard.

DISCOVERING *ILUMINA*

OTHER FEATURES

⊕ INDEX

RANDY PETERSEN is the author of *Bible Fun Stuff* and *The Family Book of Bible Fun* (Tyndale House). Basically, if it's fun and it has to do with the Bible, Randy is all over it. He has also written or cowritten more than 30 other books about topics including church history, Bible study, sports, and self-help. He wears many hats at his Methodist church in New Jersey: Bible teacher, fill-in preacher, drama team leader, and softball second baseman. In his spare time he acts, directs, and teaches acting in local theaters. Randy has been involved in *iLumina* nearly from the start, writing parts of the Time Travel and Encyclopedia sections, as well as the captions for the Virtual Tours and Points in Time.

JEREMY TAYLOR is an editor at Tyndale House Publishers and has been a member of the *iLumina* development team since the concept was born. He has been heavily involved in the content development, database preparation, and programming management for both *iLumina* and *iLumina Gold*. When he's not working on iLumina-related projects, Jeremy edits specialty Bibles and Bible-reference books and helps oversee the Bible editorial team at Tyndale. Jeremy is also responsible for the first "secret" of *iLumina*—a picture of his daughter Bethany is hidden in the first release of *iLumina*. Jeremy lives with his wife, Nancy, and their two daughters, Bethany and Alison, in Wheaton, Illinois.